DOG SHOWING

An Owner's Guide

DOG SHOWING

An Owner's Guide

by

Connie Vanacore

New York

Howell Book House
Macmillan General Reference
A Simon & Schuster Macmillan Company
1633 Broadway
New York, NY 10019-6785

Library of Congress Cataloging-in-Publication Data
Vanacore, Connie.
Dog showing : an owner's guide / by Connie Vanacore.
p. cm.
ISBN 0-87605-524-2
1. Dogs--Showing. I. Title.
SF425.V36 1990
636.7'0888--dc20 90-42614
CIP

10 9 8 7 6

Printed in the United States of America

To Fred,
who made it all possible

Contents

	Introduction	ix
1.	Getting Started and Setting Goals	1
2.	The Sport—Learning How It Works	7
3.	The Right Dog for You	19
4.	Looking at a Litter	29
5.	Health and Maintenance of a Show Dog	35
6.	Grooming the Show Dog	45
7.	Training the Show Dog	61
8.	Preparing for the Show Ring	79
9.	Plan, Pack, Go!	83
10.	Just Before the Show	97
11.	At the Show	103
12.	Sportsmanship	117
13.	The Career of the Show Dog	121
14.	Junior Showmanship: The Next Generation	133

15. The Professional Handler 141

Appendix 151

Glossary 161

Introduction

DOG SHOWS have been in existence for hundreds of years, organized informally by men who owned dogs for hunting, protection, herding or even ridding the premises of rats. A group would gather, some with dogs at their sides, at the local pub, and a wager would ensue. A bet would be placed on the dog who was the swiftest, the bravest, or the most adept at the work the dog was bred to do. Gradually these get-togethers evolved into meetings of breeders who compared their stock against that of their neighbors. Impartial arbiters were brought in, and in that manner the first dog shows were organized.

Dogs had been categorized into recognizable breeds as early as the sixteenth century, when an English physician named John Caius wrote a treatise in Latin describing six varieties. They included sight and scent hounds, land and water spaniels and setters, working terriers and fighting terriers, mastiffs and herding dogs. The first recorded dog show, however, took place in Newcastle-on-Tyne, England, on June 28 and 29, 1859. There were sixty entries for Pointers and Setters only. Gradually shows were held for other breeds in addition to gun dogs, and as the interest in the sport in England increased, the Kennel Club of England was founded, in 1873.

The first dog show in the United States was the Westminster Kennel Club, held in 1877, with more than thirty-five breeds represented. As purebred dog activity became popular here, the American Kennel Club was founded, in 1884.

The AKC was established as a registry body to maintain the breeding records of purebred dogs. It is still the primary registry for dogs in the United States, and the basic governing organization for all purebred dog activity. In 1887 the AKC began registering dogs and keeping a stud book, and as of today more than 30 million dogs have been registered with this governing body. The AKC recognizes 130 breeds of dogs, and registers in excess of 1.2 million dogs per year in its Stud Book. It is the largest registry body for dogs in the world.

To be eligible for registry in the AKC Stud Book, a dog must be able to prove a purebred lineage for three generations.

The AKC is the second-oldest amateur sport governing body in the United States, three years junior to the United States Lawn Tennis Association.

The original goal of the AKC, one it adheres to, to this day, was to set up a uniform code of rules so that anyone entering a dog in an AKC-licensed event anywhere in the country would be competing under equal conditions.

In addition to keeping the registration records, the AKC oversees over seven thousand events, including Dog Shows, Obedience Trials, field trials, hunting tests, Coonhound hunts and sanctioned matches in all these areas.

In the first eight months of 1989 there were 2,953 dog shows held, with 1,235,728 dogs exhibited at these shows. With the exception of Little League baseball, dog shows involve the largest number of amateur participants of any organized sport.

In this book, we hope to provide the reader with information on how to enjoy the world of dog showing. Every activity has its rules to live by. This book will give you those rules, and enable you to enter the world of the purebred dog.

1

Getting Started and Setting Goals

ALMOST EVERYONE who is "in dogs" began as a rank novice. Unless you were born into a family that raised dogs, or were associated with a small number of professional handlers, dog showing comes about almost by accident. Generally, people buy their first dog as a pet, sometimes from a breeder, sometimes from a pet shop. On occasion, people rescue dogs from shelters or pounds, and if it happens to be a purebred, they may become interested through that avenue.

Sometimes people become involved in Conformation competition through the Obedience rings. People who buy dogs often want them to be trained, so they go to obedience classes in their communities. Sometimes these are held by dog clubs that also hold Obedience Trials. After attending classes and a few trials, some may become interested in showing their dogs, as well as competing in Obedience. Indeed, many exhibitors begin in the Obedience ring. Obedience is an excellent way to build a rapport with your dog while at the same time learning about shows.

Dog fanciers are a very eclectic group. They range from the very wealthy to those of modest income. They include every occupation

Trophies waiting to be earned at a Keeshond Specialty. *Bernardt*

A lineup of ribbons outside an exhibitor's van shows the world that they are winners at this Specialty.

Concessions at dog shows carry all breeds in porcelain or bronze.

from professionals to blue-collar workers. Also, when dog shows began, only men belonged to clubs and only men were allowed to be delegates to the American Kennel Club, but this has changed to the point where women outnumber men in the show ring in almost every breed. Women are also well represented in most kennel clubs and are now on the Board of Directors at the American Kennel Club, and almost half of the professional handlers today are women. We will talk about the role of professionals in the sport later in this book, but many of those who now make their living showing dogs for others began as novices showing their own first dog.

MAKING YOUR GOALS REALISTIC

Once you have purchased an animal, you may become curious about the breed and want to learn more about it. You may attend a dog show, if one is happening nearby, where you will see good representatives of the breed. You may decide that your pet looks as good as these, and bring it along for a breeder to evaluate, or you may realize that your pet, no matter how lovable, is not a good enough specimen of its breed for competition.

Only you can answer the question: "What do you wish to achieve in the show ring?"

The obvious answer is that you will go to win. No one enters competition to lose, but that is really just the beginning. People show dogs to some judges because they value their opinions. Judging dogs is the most subjective of all sports, and the dog that one judge loves the next judge may hate. That is why a dog may win one day and lose the next. Or, in a well-worn dog show expression, "One day chicken, the next day feathers." One has to be able to be a good loser, as well as a good winner, in the show ring.

So, you go to win, or you go because you respect the opinion of a certain judge. What is it that you want to win? Will you be thrilled with a blue ribbon in the Puppy class, or would you like to win something more? Will finishing a championship be enough? It is for the majority of show goers. Most people go because they believe their dog is good enough to be a champion, and once it achieves that goal, they retire it from the ring.

For some people, however, that is not sufficient. Their goal may be to win Groups and Bests in Show. They may feel their dog is good enough to win over any competition, and they will take whatever

Show dogs are friends, too. (English Springer Spaniel)

Overview of an outdoor show

steps are necessary to show that dog in hopes of reaching the top. They may want their dog to be the top-winning dog in their breed for that year, or the top-winning dog in the history of their breed. They may want to win the National Specialty, or to win Westminster. All of these goals are different, but all of them require a dedication to the sport and the hard work that goes with it.

Dog showing is not all that easy. Conditions are often less than ideal, either outdoors in the rain, cold or heat, or indoors in the crowded, overheated or freezing-cold buildings that serve as show sites for some clubs. Having clear goals helps to define what you need to do and how to attain them.

In setting your goals, one thing is vital. The first lesson for any show goer is to realize that no dog is perfect, and that to recognize your dog's faults is a benefit, not a sin. If you have one dog to show, set your goals to fit that dog. If the dog is good enough to show, then it should be good enough to win a championship. Your dog may not be of sufficient quality to go on to higher achievements, but after you have been in the ring for a while, you should be able to recognize strengths and weaknesses. Setting realistic goals is one of the secrets of being a happy competitor. "Kennel blindness" can affect even the most seasoned exhibitor, and it makes for disillusionment and poor sportsmanship, both unbecoming attributes in the show ring. For most people dog showing is a hobby, and setting goals makes that hobby fun and more interesting, too.

Winning with a Briard makes this handler's day complete.

2

The Sport—Learning How It Works

THE AMERICAN KENNEL CLUB is the governing body for most purebred dog activities. Championship points awarded at AKC functions are those coveted by exhibitors and breeders as proof that their dogs are of superior quality.

The American Kennel Club is composed of Member clubs that send delegates to represent them at regularly scheduled meetings. Delegates select the AKC board of directors by ballot, and that Board runs the business of the Club. The president of the American Kennel Club must be a delegate before he or she can be selected by the board. The American Kennel Club is located in New York City at 51 Madison Avenue, and it employs a staff of four hundred to oversee registrations, Performance Events and investigations into improper conduct by breeders, exhibitors or judges; judges' education and credentials, and various other duties associated with the sport.

In addition to the Stud Book, the AKC publishes a monthly magazine, the *AKC Gazette.* It contains articles and information on all facets of the dog fancy, and each issue contains a separate section listing every dog show and its judging panel for several months in advance. There is also a separate awards section that lists every win of every dog exhibited throughout the country during the time period covered.

The structure of dog shows, in accordance with AKC regulations, is the same in all parts of the country. The variations occur when show-giving clubs decide to put on special events in addition to the basic format. These may include Obedience, Herding, Weight Pulling, bird dog or Agility demonstrations. Sometimes local K-9 Corps are invited to demonstrate their dogs' prowess.

Clubs may hold up to two licensed shows during the course of one year, for which they must apply to the Kennel Club. In addition, all-breed clubs—that is, clubs whose members represent many different breeds of dogs—must hold one match show and engage in some public education endeavor in their communities during the course of a year. Clubs may choose their own judges for their shows, from a roster of judges approved by the AKC to judge those breeds.

There are three types of events at which people can show their dogs. The first is a match show. Match shows are given by both licensed clubs and clubs hoping to be licensed by the AKC. Match shows generally are held according to the same rules as other shows, but no championship points are awarded at them, since they are usually informal gatherings for the purpose of giving inexperienced dogs and inexperienced handlers the opportunity to practice. Sometimes one sees a puppy with an owner who has been around the rings before, but often both dog and handler are learning together. Match shows are held by both all-breed clubs and Specialty clubs. The latter are clubs formed by fanciers of one specific breed to protect and enhance that breed.

The second type of show is a licensed all-breed show at which championship points may be awarded. Any or all of the 130 registrable breeds may be represented at an all-breed show. Championship points are determined by the number of dogs present in any given breed on that day. The AKC establishes the point system each May for the nine regions throughout the United States. The point scale is reached by determining how many dogs in each breed are shown throughout the year in a particular region.

In order to become a champion a dog must win fifteen points by defeating all other dogs of its sex in its breed at the shows it has entered. The fifteen points must include two shows at which three

This Norwich Terrier awaits its owner's return. *Satriale*

points or more are awarded, and these must be under different judges. Three-point-or-better shows are called majors. The least number of points that can be awarded is one and the most is five. Dogs must defeat at least one other dog in their breed in order to win the minimum. The "major" wins of three points or more are determined by the number in competition in each breed. In breeds where entries are traditionally large, the number required for a major is correspondingly high.

For instance, Golden Retrievers require anywhere from seventeen to nineteen dogs competing in order to win a major, whereas a less popular breed, such as a Lakeland Terrier, requires only four dogs in competition for a major. This does not mean it is easier to get major points in these breeds, because often there are too few dogs entered to qualify for major points. The AKC tries to assign points in a region so that no more than 20 percent of all the shows in that region carry major points. The reason for this is to discourage dogs who are not truly worthy of becoming champions from garnering major points.

One must go back to the reason for holding dog shows to appreciate this. Dogs shows were originally the means by which breeders evaluated their best breeding stock. Today, winning with a good dog is more complicated, and perhaps the motives not as clear-cut, but the reasoning behind the awarding of championship points remains the same. As an addition to this point, spayed bitches and neutered dogs are ineligible for competition, as are any dogs whose appearance has been changed by artificial means. This would include dogs whose ears have been fixed to either stand up or fold over, as the Standards require, although tail docking and ear cropping as permitted or required by breed Standards are not included in this rule. It would include dogs whose coats have been dyed a different color, tailsets that have been altered to better conform to the Standard, teeth that have been braced to make a better bite, eyelids that have been surgically corrected or any other surgically or cosmetically introduced alterations. Generally, exhibitors adhere to the rules, because they believe that breeding and showing a good specimen is the honorable thing to do. There are the few "bad apples," but their deceit is discovered in the next generations, when the dog they have shown and bred produces its faults.

The whole world of purebred dogs, from the registration of litters to showing dogs, is based on trust. Although the AKC has the means and the power to suspend individuals who break the rules, basically it comes down to breeders and exhibitors doing the right thing, and for the most part they do.

The third type of show in which you can enter your dog is the Specialty show. This is a show organized by a club representing one breed of dog. Many breed clubs hold one National Specialty show during the year, which is organized by the national club. The national club, such as the Golden Retriever Club of America or the Irish Setter Club of America, is the Parent club for the breed. There are usually several local breed clubs that are affiliated with the Parent club, and they may hold one or two Specialties during a year, as well as matches or other educational events for their members and for the public at large.

Specialty clubs often offer Sweepstakes or Futurity competitions with their shows. Sweepstakes classes are organized the same as regular classes, except that they are open to dogs 18 months and under. Classes are offered for dogs and bitches for puppies six to nine months, nine to twelve months, twelve to fifteen months, fifteen to eighteen months. The winners of these classes compete for Best in Sweepstakes and Best of Opposite Sex to Best in Sweepstakes. Prize money is awarded according to the number of entries in each class.

Futurities are offered by some clubs in order to showcase the breeders. Litters of puppies are nominated when they are born, and a designated number of puppies in each litter must be shown. Classes are divided by age and sex and prize money distributed according to the number of entries.

HOW DOG SHOWS ARE ORGANIZED

The vast majority of all-breed shows are organized according to the following pattern. Competition begins at the breed level. Classes are divided between dogs and bitches, with the exception of the class for champions, called Specials, in which both sexes are judged together. Dogs are judged before bitches in almost every case. Classes are usually offered in the following categories:

Puppy

For animals six months old to under twelve months old. This class is sometimes divided into six months to under nine months, nine months to under twelve months. Your puppy can be six months on

Socializing at an outdoor show

Outdoor spectators

Indoor spectators

the day of the show to qualify, and one day short of twelve months to still be included in the puppy class.

12 months to 18 months: The same stipulations apply for this class as for Puppy class. This class is only offered at Specialties.

Novice

For animals who have never earned a first-place in another adult class. They may remain in this class until they receive three first-place ribbons, after which they are no longer eligible. This class is regarded as a first step in experience. The dogs are usually young and not considered to be ready for serious competition.

Bred by Exhibitor

This class is open to dogs or bitches owned and shown by the breeder. Winning points from this class is considered to be a prestigious win. Bred-by classes at Specialties are looked upon as showcases for what a breeder can produce. At all-breed shows, the Bred-by class is not often large because judges tend to look to the Open class for their Winners Dog and Winners Bitch.

American Bred

This class is open to animals of any age as long as they were bred in the United States. This class is used by exhibitors with fairly mature dogs because it is usually smaller than the Open class, and they believe judges have a better opportunity to spot a likely winner in the class. Whether this is true or not depends entirely on the judge. The origin of the American Bred class traces back to the time early in the twentieth century when most show stock was imported from England. In order to provide a showcase for those second-generation dogs who were born in the United States, this class was created.

Open

This class is for mature animals, who should have had some ring experience. They are usually at least two years old, and one often sees dogs three, four or even five years old in the Open class. Some breeds, especially the large breeds, take a long time to mature, and therefore you will see older animals in this class.

The judge evaluates each class and places winners from first to fourth place in each, if he or she feels the dogs are worthy of winning ribbons. After all the classes in each sex are placed, the winners of all the classes in each sex compete for Winners Dog and Winners Bitch. These two are the only ones who receive championship points. After both are selected, the judge will award a Reserve Winners Dog and a Reserve Winners Bitch.

Winners Dog and Winners Bitch then enter competition with dogs who have already finished their championships. These are called "Specials," and they compete for Best of Breed. The judge will select a Best of Breed, Best of Opposite Sex to Best of Breed and a Best of Winners, which can be either the Winners Dog or the Winners Bitch. Sometimes one of the Winners will be chosen Best of Breed over the Specials.

At Specialty shows, the competition stops there. Best of Breed at either a local or a National Specialty is a highly coveted award.

At all-breed shows, competition moves from the breed level to the Group level. There are seven groups recognized by the American Kennel Club. They are Sporting, Hound, Working, Terrier, Toy, Non-Sporting and Herding. Best of Breed in each breed competes for placement in its respective group. The judges will award first through fourth in all seven Groups. Then the winners of the seven Groups compete for Best in Show. A win at any level is a great achievement for the dog fancier, and the reason why people go to shows week after week throughout the year.

BENCHED AND UNBENCHED SHOWS

There are a few other distinctions between the types of shows. One is the benched vs. the unbenched show. When dog shows were first organized, all were benched. That is, benches or stalls are provided by the show-giving club and dogs are required to be on display for the public when they are not actually being shown for a prescribed number of hours. Westminster, the first dog show in America, is now one of the few remaining benched shows in this country. Other benched shows are Detroit Kennel Club, Philadelphia Kennel Club, International Kennel Club in Chicago and Golden Gate Kennel Club in San Francisco. Almost all other dog shows are unbenched. That means dogs are required only to be present during the time they are being shown, and are free to leave as soon as the judging is over. Devotees of the benched show believe that some of

The benching area is a place to sit and chat. *Satriale*

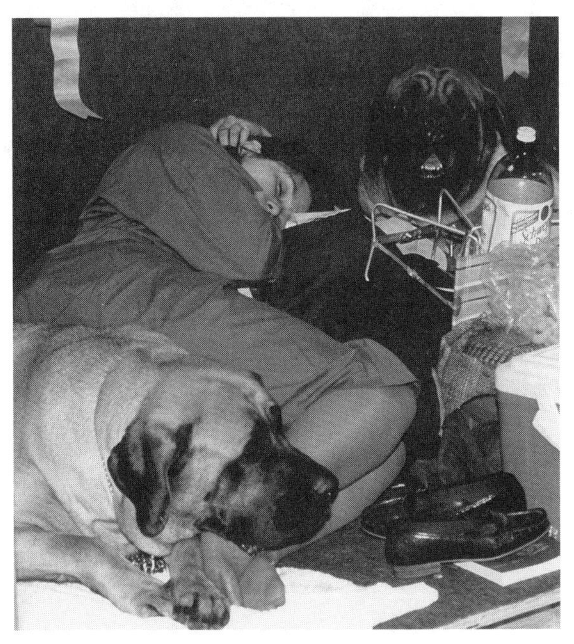
Sometimes the bench is a place for sleeping... *Satriale*

. . . or just being companions.

the most knowledgeable and caring dog people were developed during the days when exhibitors spent long hours on the benches with their dogs. There the newcomers were able to learn and mingle with the top breeders and exhibitors in the country. They were able to compare notes about breed type and structure and were able to see the dogs, not only of their own breed, but of all breeds, in an atmosphere most conducive to knowledge.

The costs of putting on a benched show and the convenience for exhibitors who wanted to be in and out and on their way home have spelled the near demise of the benched show. In its place have come cluster shows, a development born out of the gasoline shortage of the 1970s, when exhibitors found it increasingly difficult to drive long distances from one show to another over a weekend. At that point, the AKC allowed clubs to combine at a single show site and hold several shows on the same grounds. There exhibitors get together after the shows and share information, as well as comradery, especially among those who travel in motor homes. The dog show crowd has become an increasingly mobile group, going from show to show much the way tourists travel from one campground to another from week to week.

One other distinction needs to be made in facilities—the outdoor show vs. the indoor show. In many parts of the country the dog show seasons are divided among the two. In late spring, summer and fall, shows move outside to parks or other large open spaces, where exhibitors are provided with rings partially shaded by tents. Some of the best shows in the country, such as Santa Barbara Kennel Club on the West Coast and Westchester Kennel Club in the East, are outdoor shows.

In some areas, the climate simply does not permit outdoor shows during much of the year, and these venues are held in convention centers, schools or other large indoor facilities. Among the biggest are the shows held in the Astro Hall in Houston in August. Acres of air-conditioned rings, exercise areas and vendors selling pet-related products make these shows very popular with exhibitors and the public.

Dog shows are a way of getting the whole family, including the family dog, involved in a sport. They may love the competition, pitting their skills in showing against others. They may use shows as an excuse to travel, visiting breeders in various parts of the country, attending shows anywhere in the United States, and even Mexico and Canada.

Ch. Blackburn's Baronof Brutus. The "King of Terriers" can clown with the best of them.
Lindsey

3

The Right Dog for You

THE COMMON WISDOM is that men marry their mothers and dogs look like their owners. People are attracted to the familiar, and it is not so much that after living together for a period of time dogs and owners grow closer in appearance, but the fact that people select their pets for traits that appeal to their own personalities. In those instances where a dog's breed type is very dissimilar to its owner's temperament, the marriage often proves unhappy. For an owner who wants to show his dog, marriage is not too strong a word. In order to create a winning combination in the show ring, dog and master must be bonded together. They must be a team. That is one reason why choosing the right breed is an essential first step to any success in the show ring.

Purchasing a dog, whether for pet or for show, should be considered as one of the most important decisions you make in your life. Once you own a dog, it becomes your responsibility to care for it, to train it, to socialize it in the home and in the neighborhood, and to prepare to do all these things over a long period of time. Dogs are not stuffed animals, to be discarded as soon as the child tires of them, nor are they used cars to be traded in after a few years of wear. Dogs are truly long-term investments, which will become more valuable directly in proportion to the amount of interest and care you put into them. Most show dogs are also treasured companions. They were purchased as pets, and long after their show careers are over, they will still be man's best friend. The show life of a show dog seldom lasts more than three years from start to finish, but a dog will live for ten, twelve or fifteen years, sometimes longer. Your dog will be at home after your kindergartner has gone off to college and the blue ribbons are faded on the mantle. There may be other show dogs in your home as the first grows older, but the choice of your first show dog may mean the difference between starting off right and quitting. The life of the average show goer is short, but it need not be. It can last for decades, as some of the most distinguished breeders can attest.

SELECTING THE RIGHT BREED

In choosing any breed, the first quality is appeal. Which breeds do you find most attractive? Are the Sporting breeds appealing with their outgoing dashing ways? How about the dignified sight hounds, or the energetic scent hounds? Do you like the spunk of the Terriers, the dedication to task of the Working dogs, or the daintiness of the Toys? What about the catch-all Non-Sporting dogs with their diverse natures, or the mother-hen personalities of the Herding dogs? Within the seven Groups recognized by the AKC, there must be just the dog for you.

After you have studied about the breeds and gone to a few dog shows, you will be ready to narrow your choice according to what your own life circumstances are. If you live in a one-room flat in the city you will not want to get a Great Dane, nor any of the breeds that absolutely must have exercise and fresh air to survive. People do own these breeds, of course, despite limiting surroundings, but they must be very dedicated to getting out with their dogs to provide them with the exercise they require.

How about hair? Are you the kind of person who blanches at the thought of balls of dog hair blowing around the floor? Is your life so full of other things that you would not have several hours a week to groom a show coat? Then a long-haired dog is not for you.

How about the rest of the family? Are they in favor of having a dog in the house? Are they willing to pitch in and help with its care

Labrador Retriever and family enjoy the day.

This Pomeranian looks out from a fenced run.

Little girls are introduced to a Shetland Sheepdog puppy.

Maybe a Beagle is right for your family.

and training? Are they attuned to sharing your interest in showing this dog? If the answers to these questions are affirmative, your logistical problems of raising a show dog will be much easier.

Are there children present or expected? Young children do better with large dogs than with tiny ones, which can be easily injured or frightened, so size should be a consideration in your selection of a puppy.

Size is also important for you, as an exhibitor. If you are a small and frail person, a Mastiff or a Rottweiler is probably not the best choice of breed to begin a show career. However, it is essential to choose a breed that you love, and overcome the difficulties in showing it as you go along.

Another decision to be made is whether to get a male or a female (to be described from now on as a dog or a bitch, in breeder's parlance). Dogs generally are more imposing at maturity. They will grow more luxurious coats; they will be bigger and have a more commanding presence. The larger breeds, however, will take longer to mature and go through the adolescent horribles, and sometimes are more difficult to train.

Bitches are generally smaller, in most breeds, somewhat easier to control, not as flashy or showy in appearance, and often shed their coats after they have been in season. This may be a problem for an exhibitor trying to win those final championship points. There are exceptions to every generality, however, and there are bitches who never lose all their coat, are very outgoing and "on stage" in the ring, and who can beat the boys at their own game quite handily.

If you think you might want to proceed beyond showing your first animal, then you should buy the best bitch you can afford. If becoming a breeder seems like too much effort, but you don't mind owning a good stud dog (also a lot of work), then perhaps you should think about purchasing a good male.

It really does come down to preference, and if you find a litter that you like, take the pick, whether it be dog or bitch.

One question that should occur to any novice early in his or her involvement in the sport is how to determine if a dog is worthy of being shown. In addition to watching other dogs and talking to people, one should obtain a copy of the "Standard of perfection" for the breed.

Every recognized breed has a Standard by which dogs are measured. The Standard has been developed by fanciers early in the development of the breed and must be accepted by the AKC and promulgated by the breed club. From time to time, as breeds evolve, Standards undergo revisions, though changing the Standard in any way is always a major undertaking for a breed club, and is done with extreme care and conservatism. Most clubs have written material about their breed, including the Standard and often an interpretation of the words of the Standard. These are available upon request from the club, sometimes free of charge, sometimes for a small fee.

In addition to the written Standard, many clubs have cooperated with the AKC in producing videos about their breeds, and these are available for rent or purchase from the AKC.

By studying these materials and watching dogs in the ring, novices will be able to get a good idea of what the breed should be, and how their dog measures up to the Standard.

WHERE TO PURCHASE A SHOW DOG

Whether you are going to buy a show dog or a pet, reputable breeders who show their dogs will try to produce the best puppies from the soundest breeding stock that they can. Therefore, your direction should be toward people who produce animals that are considered to be good representatives of the breed.

There are a few avenues to pursue in finding your show prospect. Attend dog shows where several dogs of your chosen breed are present. You will have nothing to compare if only one or two specimens are on display. However, it's a start, and from those exhibitors you might obtain the names of breeders whom you can contact.

The American Kennel Club maintains a list of club officers of every Parent club and many local clubs. You can write or call them to obtain the names of current officers. With those names in hand, you can contact one or more and get from them a list of breeders in your area. Some clubs maintain a breeders' directory, which includes those who have bred a prescribed number of litters and are eligible to be listed on an annual basis. It may be that there is no one in your area who breeds the dogs you have decided on, and you may have to travel some distance to find what you are looking for. Often breeders have waiting lists for their puppies, and if you are truly committed to a certain breeder, you will have to wait, sometimes as long as a year, to get what you want.

Selecting a Breeder

As with any major purchase, you have to do your homework. Once you have your list of names from the Parent breed club itself, try to visit several breeders. Find out what their involvement is with the sport and with the breed. If they belong to and are active in local and national breed clubs, then they usually are truly interested in the breed. Do they show their own dogs? How long have they been breeding, and how much success have they had? It is not necessary for a breeder to produce vast numbers of puppies in order to be involved and concerned for the welfare of the breed. In fact, you would most likely be better off with a breeder who produces one litter a year, sometimes less, providing those litters are well planned and well cared for.

For the novice, the best advice may be to purchase a puppy or a young dog outright and then return to the breeder for advice on guiding its show career. The fewer entanglements you get into, the more you will learn on your own, and the fewer chances there will be for misunderstandings and unhappiness. Co-ownerships are tricky. They can be more restrictive than marriage and just as difficult to terminate, should either party be unhappy. The AKC advises buyers not to co-own, if it is at all possible to get the dog you want without it.

In fairness to the breeders, co-ownerships provide a means for them to keep track of their stock, to select mates for the sires or dams when they are old enough to be bred and to let the world know that they have produced this wonderful dog. Some of the most reputable breeders will only sell bitches particularly, on "breeders' terms." That way they know how their bitches will be used, and it is the only sure way of protecting a line they have worked hard to develop.

It is important for anyone purchasing a dog, especially a show dog, to be aware of all the contingencies and to have it all written down in a contract. (Sample contracts will be found in the Appendix at the back of this book.) Some of the things that may be included are when the puppy should be shown, who will show it, who pays for entry fees and other expenses of the showing the dog. If the puppy is a male, does the breeder get stud service rights and for how long? If the puppy is a bitch, does the breeder have the right to choose the stud? Does the breeder get puppies back from the litter? For how many litters is the owner obligated to the breeder? If the dog is sold on a co-ownership, does that last forever, or is there a time limit to

This is a well-maintained kennel.

Welsh Springer and English Cocker Spaniels are exercised on gravel behind secure fences.

the arrangement? All these things should be worked out ahead of time in order to avoid conflict later on.

It is important to visit more than one kennel or private breeder in order to get an idea of the differences, and so you can make a knowledgeable decision based on your observations. All puppies are adorable, but after you have seen a few litters, you will see that some succeed where others fail.

After you have investigated the background of the breeder, and have looked at the pedigrees of the sire and dam, it is time to see the puppies themselves.

Most breeders prefer that prospective buyers not look at a litter until it is at least six weeks old. By then the puppies will have had their initial vaccinations, they are partially or completely weaned from the dam, and are running around fairly steadily on their little legs. No reputable breeder will let puppies go before eight weeks of age, and in some states it is against the law to sell puppies younger than eight weeks. If a breeder intends to keep one or more of the litter, he or she may want to hold on to the most promising puppies until they are ten or twelve weeks old. Sometimes a breeder may decide to keep the pick of the litter for several months before letting it go if it doesn't quite measure up to expectations.

When you call to make an appointment to see a litter, it is important to tell the breeder that you are interested in a show-quality puppy. If breeders think you are serious about showing the dog, they will usually go out of their way to help you select a good-quality animal. In a well-bred litter the differences between a show prospect and what is considered a "pet" are very small, and to the untutored eye practically negligible. That is why it is important to find a breeder who will evaluate the litter honestly for you.

It is practically impossible, no matter how lovely a puppy appears to be at ten weeks, to say with any certainty that it will grow up to be an outstanding show dog. Too many things can go wrong, from the genetic structure of the puppy itself, to its upbringing and training, nutrition and care. *Beware of the breeder who guarantees that a puppy will finish its championship.* The most that can be guaranteed is that the puppy is healthy, appears to be mentally sound and, for its age, is structurally correct.

Seven-and-a-half-week-old Keeshond puppies. *Thomas Cooke*

These German Wirehaired Pointer puppies show a keen interest in visitors as they look out from their pen. This eagerness will make them good prospects.

4

Looking at a Litter

YOU HAVE DONE your homework, talked to several breeders and made appointments to view their litters. Now, what do you look for when you go to visit? These guidelines, incidentally, apply whether or not you are going to buy a show puppy. Most show puppies are primarily pets, and will be pets, whether or not they star in the ring, so good health and stable temperaments are essential.

The first thing to notice, whether it is a kennel or a house, an elaborate puppy room or the family den, is sanitation. The place should look and smell clean. It should not reek of waste, nor of heavy room deodorizer masking a dirty litter. The puppies should be housed in clean surroundings, whether it be newspapers, towels, bedding or bare floors.

Fresh water should be available and if food bowls are in the pen they should be clean, showing no evidence of old crusted food.

The puppies themselves should be clean, with that distinctive sweet puppy smell. They should not be covered in filth or matted with food, and their quarters should be large enough so that their innate sense of cleanliness can be achieved. The puppies, unless they are peacefully sleeping, should be active, running and playing. They should be responsive to strangers, coming up willingly to an outstretched hand, clamoring for attention. Their eyes should be clear and bright, with no sign of congestion. Their noses should be moist

The members of this litter are beginning to go their separate ways.

These young puppies enjoy meeting a new friend.

An Irish Setter puppy is obviously happy as he romps in the grass.

These English Cocker Spaniel puppies use the buddy system to explore.

but not runny, and their bodies should be firm to the touch. They should be well covered with flesh but not flabby or soft. Their coats should be shiny and sleek.

There are two ways to look at puppies, and you should do both. The breeder may take each puppy separately and stack it for you on a grooming table so you can see its conformation compared to others in the litter. He or she may point out subtle differences that you would be unable to notice until you became more experienced. Once each puppy has been examined, it should be put on the floor or on the ground so you can see it running on its own. When all the puppies have been looked at singly, you should sit quietly and watch them play.

You will see the differences in personality come forward. Some will be the ringleaders, others the followers. Once you get your puppy home and away from its littermates, that pack personality will change somewhat, but you can get an idea from seeing them all together which will be the dominant ones and which the subservient. Matching owners and dogs according to their personalities is a very interesting way of selecting a puppy. In choosing a show puppy, most people prefer one that is outgoing and not afraid of new surroundings or of meeting new people.

The question of price is difficult. In some parts of the country a good show prospect will cost much more than in other areas. In addition, the popularity of the breed determines the price: the greater the number of puppies available, the lower the prices will be; the rarer the breed, the more expensive. There are also the "fad" breeds that are popular at the moment, and those breeders charge two or three times what other breeds cost. Litters coming from champion sires and dams cost more than others. Sometimes one sees advertisements for litters "from champion stock." That usually means nothing, except that somewhere in the distant past there was a champion.

When you look at the pedigree for a litter, if both sire and dam and many of the antecedents are champions, you can expect to pay somewhat more for the puppy. Price should not be the first consideration in purchasing a show puppy, but you can get an idea of the cost by comparing the prices of different litters.

Although no reputable breeder will guarantee a champion at ten weeks, there are some guarantees that you should be given when you purchase your puppy. It should be guaranteed to be in good health at the time of purchase, and free of any known inheritable defects. That means, if the breed is known to carry certain genetic faults, your

An eight-week-old Bichon Frise puppy contemplates his new world. *Missy*

This young English Cocker is learning what it takes to be a show dog.

purchase will not have them, to the best of the breeder's knowledge. Some breeders will take back a puppy that later displays an undesirable trait that was not evident at the time of purchase. Whatever guarantees you are promised by the breeder should be given in writing at the time of purchase.

In addition to these guarantees, you should receive a copy of the puppy's pedigree (the AKC frowns on breeders charging extra for this) and also the puppy's litter registration (the blue slip), which you then fill out and send with your fee to the AKC to register your puppy.

Many breeders send home a "care package" with the puppy, including a record of the vaccinations and stool checks the puppy has received, instructions on feeding and sometimes the breeder's own ideas on housebreaking, training and so forth. You would be well advised to follow the breeder's advice and schedule in the beginning, to avoid unnecessary upsets to the puppy in its new surroundings. Most breeders are more than happy to answer questions and to keep in touch with their puppy buyers. You, in turn, will have access to the help you will need as you develop your puppy into a show dog.

5

Health and Maintenance of a Show Dog

ALL PUPPIES, whether show prospects or not, require care and attention to enable them to grow up healthy and stable. Routine is very important to a growing dog. Puppies will go through stages in which their personalities develop along with their bodies, and their intake of food and output of energy must keep pace. A healthy puppy will grow into a healthy show dog.

DIET

A high-quality diet is essential to develop strong bones and good structure. The most perfectly made dog will never reach its potential without proper nutrition. A well-balanced commercial diet of kibble and meat or of home-prepared grains and meat should be fed to a growing dog several times a day. If you feed a recognized brand, there should be no need for additional supplements. In fact, the addition of calcium, vitamin D and/or vitamin E or A could seriously affect the proper development of the long bones and cause structural deficiencies that cannot be reversed. *In feeding puppies, more is not better.*

Puppies do better on some foods than others, and you may have to experiment a bit at a time to find just the right formula for your dog. Read the labels. For instance, if you feed a balanced kibble designed for puppies, you do not need to supplement that with a complete canned-meat dinner. You might wish to add a little meat for flavor, and there are canned meats that contain no additional cereal and fillers. There are designer dog foods for every owner's palate and pocketbook. Veterinary research indicates that cheaper is not better when it comes to dog foods, as many generic or supermarket chain labels are deficient in some of the essential trace elements. However, that does not mean that you must buy the most expensive product in order to provide optimum nutrition for your growing dog. There is a bewildering array of foods available to the consumer, but the majority of exhibitors and kennel owners buy their food at pet or feed supply outlets, preferring brands that are not available on the supermarket shelves.

A balanced diet is one on which your puppy gains a steady amount of growth and weight per week. Palatability is important. The best food in the world is useless if the puppy won't eat it. Digestibility is another important aspect. Some foods are more completely utilized by the dog, which means that less waste is produced. Stools should be firm and small. Copious stools indicate that the food is not being used by the dog's body as efficiently as it should be. Coat condition is another indication of how well the dog is being maintained on the diet you are feeding. Dry coats, flaky skin, lack of hair growth are possible signs of a deficient diet. There are, of course, other reasons for unthriftiness and poor hair quality.

INTESTINAL PARASITES

Dog owners spend a great deal of time looking down. That is because the production, cleanup and analysis of stools is a very important component of maintaining a healthy dog. Many puppies have intestinal parasites that they acquire either through the mother, prenatally, or through the mother's milk, if she has not been properly maintained. Hookworms and roundworms are the most commonly

Nutrition is important at every stage of life.

seen intestinal varieties, and they can be transmitted through the placenta or from the surroundings. Both live in the soil. Roundworms are those most usually associated with puppies, and they can be easily eliminated with proper medication.

Even though the breeder has wormed the puppies before they leave for their new homes, it is a good idea to take a stool sample to your veterinarian just to be sure. In addition to hookworms and roundworms, whipworms can be picked up from the ground; these are difficult to eradicate and very debilitating to the dog. Any burden of parasites that a puppy carries will sap its strength and vigor and will prevent it from being in optimum health. Worms are a common cause of dry skin and coat, intestinal upsets and poor stools. Any time you see stools containing mucus or blood, you should suspect intestinal parasites. Intermittent diarrhea or watery stools are another indication that parasites may be present. You must treat the dog according to the veterinarian's instructions, and you must treat the surroundings as well as possible. Clean up bedding, scrub down floors with hot water and chlorine bleach and keep the outside picked up. Do not allow stools to accumulate in kennel runs or yards because you are asking for reinfection.

Parasites such as hookworms or whipworms suck blood from a dog's intestinal tract, and if left untreated the dog will become anemic. They are especially dangerous in young puppies, where they can prove fatal.

EXTERNAL PARASITES

Internal cleanliness must be matched in the show puppy with external cleanliness. Fleas are the biggest curse of the dog owner because of damage they do to skin and coat. Any prospective show fancier must have fleas under control. Flea allergy dermatitis is the most common skin disease in the world, and the source of almost half of a veterinarian's business. Itch leads to scratch leads to chew leads to destruction of coat and skin, ultimately leading to bacterial infection. Controlling fleas in some areas of the country, especially in the southeast, is a most difficult problem, but in order to show dogs in those warm, moist climates, it must be done. A regular routine of spraying yard and house, bathing and dipping the dogs can eliminate fleas in the immediate environment. Dedicated breeders prove that it can be done, but it takes constant vigilance. A dog under constant attack by fleas will never be at its best, either mentally or physically.

Another increasingly dangerous parasite is the tick. Ticks carry diseases such as Rocky Mountain spotted fever, tularemia and Lyme disease. Lyme disease has become the number-one cause of serious pest-related illness to both dog and man in the country. This disease is carried by the deer tick, not by wood or brown dog ticks, which carry the other illnesses. The deer tick is so tiny you can barely see it, and it has spread throughout the United States with unprecedented speed in the past five years. The deer tick is borne by deer, but also by field mice and other creatures of the woods and fields. This is a particularly dangerous parasite because the effects of being bitten by a tick carrying the spirochete that transmits Lyme disease are serious and long lasting. If you or your dog has been exposed to ticks, be aware of symptoms such as lameness, fever and anorexia. In people, the symptoms may begin with a circular red rash at the site of the tick bite. The rash may spread and then disappear, and other symptoms may show up weeks or months later. In both people and dogs, if the symptoms are left untreated, complications to heart and liver may occur. Rheumatoid arthritis has been linked to Lyme disease, and in people loss of memory and other neurological symptoms have been seen. Any tick bite should be treated as serious and a potential harbinger of devastating illness. Blood tests may detect the presence of the spirochete, but they are not always accurate. If Lyme disease is suspected, several blood tests over a period of days or weeks should be taken.

Antiobiotics administered over an extended period of time are usually successful in treating the disease. However, unless diagnosed and treated promptly, Lyme disease may have lasting effects.

VACCINATIONS

Your puppy will come to you having had a series of vaccinations. You should obtain from the breeder a record of exactly what shots have been given and when they have been administered. Take this record to your veterinarian so he can determine when the next vaccinations are due.

Distemper, hepatitis, leptospirosis and parainfluenza shots are usually given together in a series completed by the time the puppy is sixteen weeks old. Sometimes parvovirus vaccinations are given at the same time, though some veterinarians prefer to separate the parvovirus shots from the others. Giving all the shots together is a lot for the puppy's immune system to handle at once. Some veterinarians recommend that Parvo shots should be given at two week intervals until the puppy is twenty weeks old.

Show dogs are exposed to a great many more diseases than most other pets, and therefore it is important to keep the vaccinations current. A dog in optimum health that is properly immunized will have a much better chance of warding off diseases that can be contracted at shows. Any time many animals are confined in close quarters, the risk of contracting illnesses is great. You can minimize the dangers by keeping your dog away from others as much as possible. Do not allow it to sniff other dogs or their excrement. Exercise your dog away from others, and when you are showing your dog regularly, have stool checks done monthly.

The most commonly transmitted diseases at dog shows are intestinal viruses and respiratory ailments. Parvovirus and coronavirus were first spread largely throughout the United States by show dogs in close contact, bringing the viruses home and spreading them throughout the kennel and the neighborhood. Both of these diseases are largely controlled now through vaccinations. However, other intestinal viruses are capable of being spread through contact with infected dogs or feces. Any intestinal upset should be considered serious, especially in young puppies, and should be treated without delay.

In young puppies and in older dogs dehydration is a very rapid and debilitating condition brought about by diarrhea or vomiting. If dehydration is left uncontrolled for as few as twenty-four hours, a puppy can be seriously compromised and even die. Antidiarrheal medication and intravenous fluids are often needed by the young or by the geriatric dog to save its life.

Respiratory infections are the other commonly spread diseases. "Kennel cough," a dry, hacking cough, is easily transmitted from one dog to another. It is usually a self-limiting disease, but the animal will feel poorly, lack pep and lack appetite. Respiratory illness that involves runny noses, runny eyes or production of mucus can be treated with antibiotics.

Any dog that shows evidence of illness should be isolated from

This Newfoundland learns to trot on a lead . . .

but he prefers swimming for his exercise.

its kennel mates, and should certainly not be taken out to shows or around other dogs where it can spread disease.

FITNESS

Exercise is very important for a growing dog. All breeds, from Toys to giants, need exercise to benefit mentally as well as physically. Puppies should be encouraged to run, to play, to explore and to investigate new places and new things. Puppies should not be forced into more exercise than their growing bones can handle, but they should be given the opportunity every day to get themselves happily exhausted. Some dogs, such as the Sporting or Terrier breeds, have high energy levels, and these will need more exercise than some of the lap dogs. Even the little creatures, however, will be in better health if they are physically fit.

As the puppy grows and develops, some controlled exercise can be added, such as learning to trot on a lead. Since trotting is what it will have to do in the show ring, it is useful to start the pup off at home, learning the coordination that is needed to trot with a long and free stride. Puppies naturally like to canter or gallop, and a sustained trot only comes with maturity. Starting them off gradually when they are young will make it easier for them later on.

Exercise must be part of the daily routine, and the puppy should be kept in an area big enough so it can run freely, without coming up short to a fence. Dogs will adjust their stride to the physical space provided for them. If your puppy is always kept in a short run, it will never be able to adapt its stride to its full potential. Sometimes dogs that pitty-pat around the show ring are the product of a constricted environment. To give your show puppy every advantage, make sure it is exercised properly.

Some people enjoy bike riding or jogging with their dogs. This type of exercise is not beneficial to a young puppy. Jogging for long distances on pavement or other hard surfaces will break down the pasterns and load up the shoulders, so the dog will never look good. Limited jogging can be started when the dog is fully grown, at about two years of age, but while the dog is growing, other forms of exercise are more suitable. Walking, free running, hunting, swimming, playing ball at the dog's own pace will give it all the exercise it needs without injuring bones, tendons and muscles. Avoid exercise that uses the same muscles repetitively over a long period of time until the dog is mature.

Maintaining a show puppy is no different than caring for any pet. You must be ahead of problems, not catching up to them. Preventing rather than treating saves time and money, and keeps that show puppy in top shape.

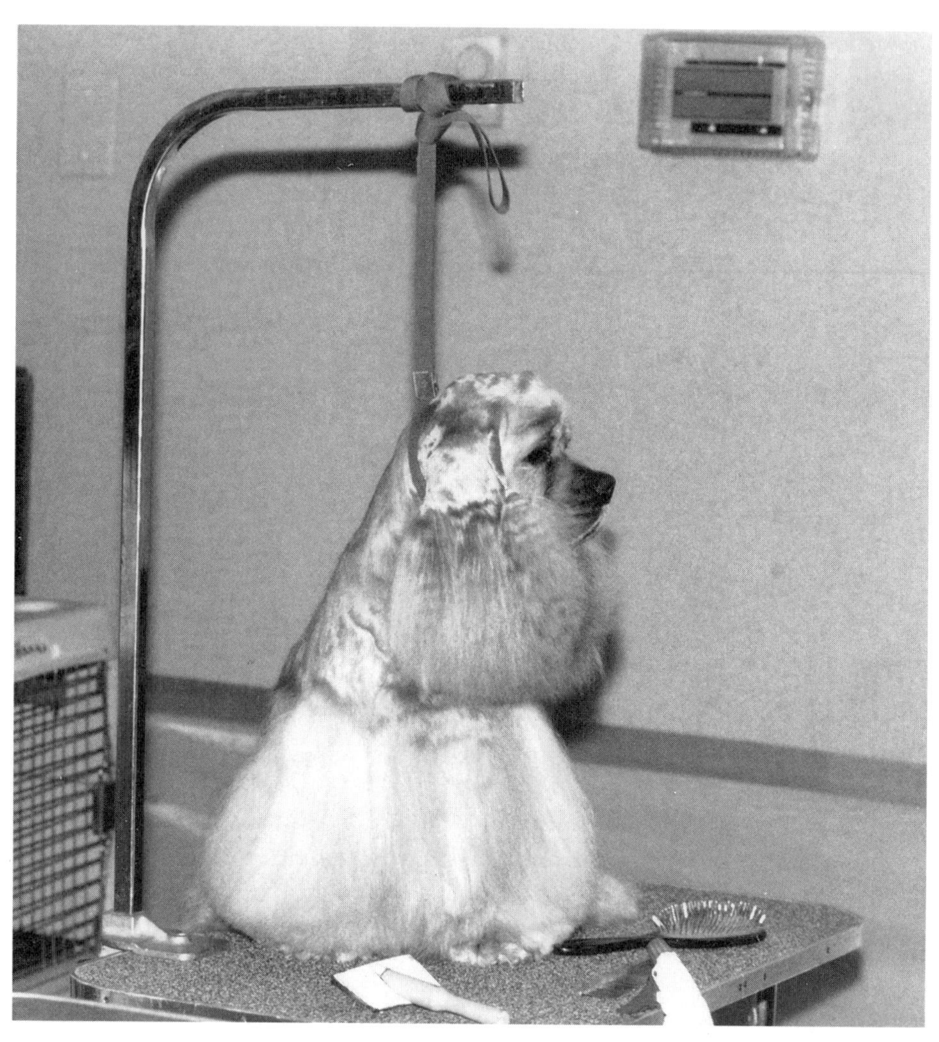

This Cocker Spaniel on its grooming table awaits application of pin brush and slicker. Grooming arm and lead hold dog on the table.

6

Grooming the Show Dog

GROOMING YOUR DOG is a lifelong process, whether or not you intend to ever show the dog. It is one of the best ways to observe the state of your dog's health, from ears to tail.

Grooming is more than merely brushing the coat once or twice a week. It involves basic maintenance before you ever get to the fine points of show trimming. Grooming is part of health care because it involves trimming the nails, cleaning the ears, brushing and scaling the teeth, bathing and examining the skin for the signs of infection, parasites, dryness, scaling or discoloration that are indications of trouble.

Dogs who have become accustomed to the grooming table and to being handled and brushed from the time they are small look forward to their time with their masters. Grooming is one of the most primitive instincts of man and animals. Although we use sophisticated tools to groom our pets, dogs and cats groom themselves and each other. The most common expressions of social grooming are found among the great apes, although most other animals engage in grooming activity.

Grooming is a great way to become closer to your dog. By the

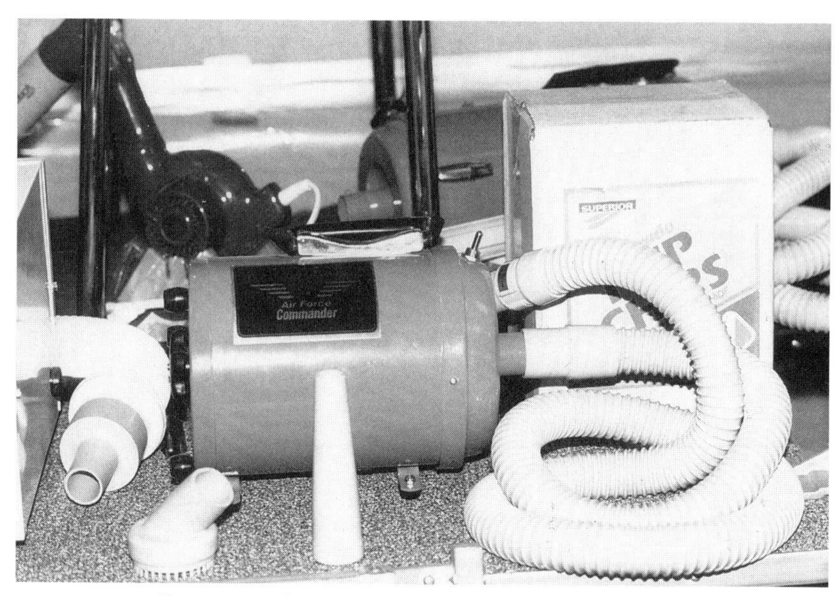

Air pressure blower and hand-held drier are useful at shows.

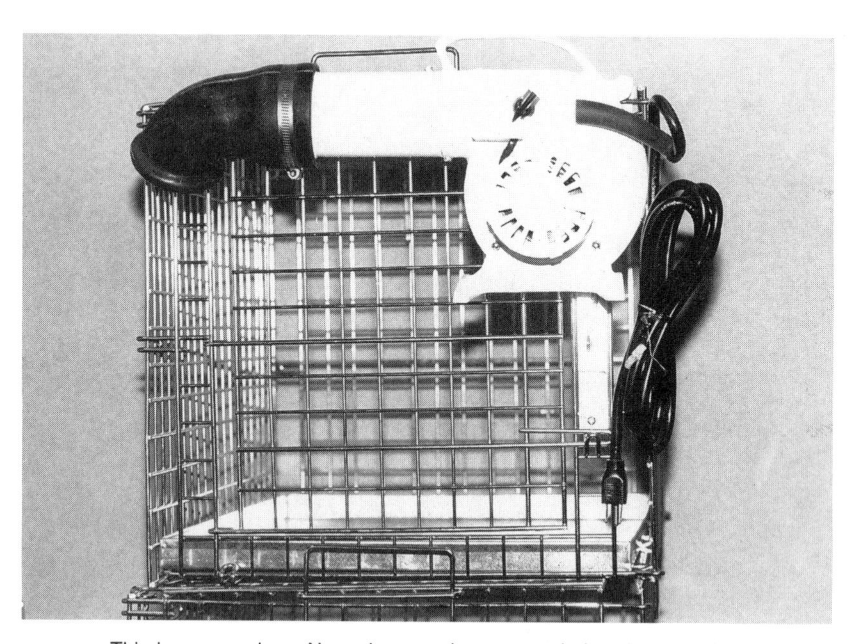

This is a cage dryer. Never leave a dog unattended under one of these.

There are grooming products for every need.

This grooming box has room for clipper and show leads. Spray bottle hangs from the crate.

stroking, preening and attention you give it during the times it is being groomed you are establishing close bonds. It is also a relaxing way to spend a couple of hours. Although short-haired dogs require far less work with their hair than long-coated breeds, there is still a need for brushing, bathing and examination.

Grooming long coats, or those that require trimming for the show ring, demands total concentration. That, in itself, is a relaxing activity that can transport you away from the daily cares while you attend to your closest companion. Grooming is a great way to take out frustrations and to dream of this perfect dog you are creating with shears and brush.

This type of grooming activity is only successful if you have a dog who enjoys the attention, has patience and is accustomed to spending time on the grooming table. You must develop this habit from puppyhood. Dogs can be groomed as soon as they are able to stand up, and a few minutes a day on the table, being stroked with a soft brush, will establish good feelings about the whole routine.

TOOLS OF THE TRADE

Different grooming tools are needed for different types of hair, but in all cases, except for the giant breeds, such as Great Danes, Irish Wolfhounds and Scottish Deerhounds, a grooming table is a must. It can be cut down with short legs for the large breeds, or bought with tall legs for the small breeds. Any table will do as long as it is sturdy and covered with nonslip material. You can purchase collapsible grooming tables in various sizes that you can carry to shows. Some, which come with wheels, can be turned into a dolly for carrying the other paraphernalia you will need when you go to a dog show.

The table should be large enough to allow the dog to lie down comfortably, as many dogs are groomed lying first on one side and then the other, and it should be of a height that is comfortable for your back. Dogs should be helped onto and off the table. Dogs who jump off grooming tables can injure their shoulders, and there is nothing more discouraging than to see your dog limp up to the ring after you have spent countless hours preparing for a show.

Never leave your dog unattended on a grooming table. Sometimes one sees dogs at shows sitting on their tables, without anyone nearby. This is a risky and dangerous habit. Many grooming tables are equipped with metal arms, which are attached to slip collars. Dogs left with their heads in the collars are particularly prone to accidents. The dog can slip off the table, or decide to jump off to see some enticing female nearby and break its neck. There are collars that will snap open under pressure, but that is no guarantee that a dog cannot injure itself in some other way. It is a prime rule to always attend to your dog while it is on the table.

There are dozens of different types of combs, brushes, scissors, razors, clippers, strippers and whatever else one could possibly think of to prepare your dog for the show ring. They are often specific for the type of coat the breed has, but everyone needs a good metal comb and a bristle brush. From there on you will need the advice of someone in your breed to show you how to groom your dog properly.

A hair dryer is an essential grooming tool. There are many different types, from hand-held models to those which sit on a table or the larger floor models. Many are equipped with adjustable heat and blower settings, and they range in price according to the complexity and power of the machine. Dryers are essential for any of the coated breeds.

USING THE TOOLS

There are numerous tools for every part of the grooming process. The choice of tools is usually one of personal preference, influenced in part by the physical characteristics of the dog and the amount one wishes to spend in this area. Learning to use each of these tools effectively is a result of the combined efforts of observation and practice.

Nail Clipping

Toenail clipping is one of the necessities of grooming, but it often becomes a battle between dog and owner. Dogs are particularly sensitive about their feet, and cutting the nail so that it bleeds is a common mistake. The nail should be trimmed just in front of the quick, so that it is a painless process. The puppy has to learn to have its nails done, and extra care when it is small and the nails are soft will prevent agonizing sessions later on. Nails can be trimmed with a guillotine-type clipper, available in any pet supply store, or with a pincer-type clipper, also available in most outlets. They can also

This Bichon Frise is prepared for show under the grooming tent.

A Poodle is groomed outside handler's motor home.

A Bearded Collie is brushed out in the kennel.

be filed down with a circular sanding tool that attaches to some electric hair clippers. In all cases, it is important to avoid cutting into the quick, which is where the blood vessels and nerves are.

Many breeders begin to nip off the ends of the nails when the puppies are tiny, about three weeks old. Even at that age they have sharp nails that can dig into the mother's side as they nurse. If you keep the nails short from the beginning, you will have very few problems later on. Human nail clippers are satisfactory for puppies, and the nails can be done quickly and painlessly, holding the puppy on your lap. As the dog grows, this process can be done on the grooming table. It is a good idea to have some type of styptic on hand to put on the ends of the nail should you mistakenly cut into the quick.

Nails should be kept short, although in some breeds, particularly Poodles, nails are trimmed back almost to the nail bed. In most breeds it is sufficient to keep the nails trimmed so you do not hear them clicking on the floor when the dog walks. When you are showing your dog, nails should be done weekly, with just the ends taken off. For regular maintenance they can be done monthly, depending upon how short you have kept them.

Do the nails before you begin any other grooming procedure. That way the dog will realize the unpleasant part is over and it will not be concerned that you will creep up on it at any time during the session.

Ear Cleaning

Ears should be cleaned weekly with either alcohol on a cotton swab or one of the ear cleanser products available from a pet supply outlet or your veterinarian. Dogs with hanging ears, such as Spaniels or Basset Hounds, tend to develop ear infections quickly, because air cannot circulate into the ear canal. Yeast infections are common and are difficult to eradicate. Ear mites, tiny parasites that invade the ear canal, are easily transmitted from one dog to another, or from cats to dogs.

Ear problems can be suspected if the dog is constantly scratching at his ears or rubbing his ears along the furniture or on the floor. You can see black exudate in the ear canal, which is often accompanied by a strong odor. If left untended, ear infections can spread into the glands in the neck and will cause the dog great discomfort. Occasionally you will see a dog in the show ring who constantly shakes its head when the lead is placed up under the ears. Usually this is an indication that there are problems with the ears. It is surprising how often owners neglect to look inside the ears and to clean them out as part of regular maintenance.

When swabbing the ears, be sure the cotton on a swab is thick, or if the ear canal is large enough, use your finger wrapped in cotton. Do not jab into the ear canal or you may cause damage to the ear drum or the sensitive bones inside the inner ear.

If the ear infection is serious, the veterinarian may want to anesthetize the dog and irrigate the ear canal by flushing it with pressurized water.

Tooth Care

Dogs have dental problems, just the same as people do, with the exception of the fact that dogs seldom develop cavities. Probably this is because they are fed better diets than their owners. They are prone to gum disease and tartar buildup, however, and these can cause discomfort, infection and eventually loss of teeth. In a show dog, that can spell the end of its career. Although it is claimed that chewing biscuits will help remove plaque from the dog's teeth, one would have to eat a meal exclusively of biscuits in order to derive any benefit from that. Some dogs are very prone to buildup of plaque, while others never experience that problem, and diet does not appear to play a role.

To prevent the accumulation of tartar, the dog's teeth can be brushed with any toothpaste or with a paste made of baking soda and water. They don't like it much, but if it is done regularly, several times a week, they will get accustomed to it. Plaque can be removed using a human dental tool and scraping just under the gum downward toward the end of the tooth. Most accumulation occurs on the back molars, which are difficult to reach in small dogs. Small dogs and dogs with mouths that fit tightly over the gums are more prone to plaque formation, and these may need dental care by the veterinarian. Once or twice a year the teeth may need to be professionally cleaned. This is usually done under anesthesia or tranquilization because the dog will not submit willingly to the procedure.

Dogs with diseased gums often find it difficult to chew, and one clue for the owner to a possible dental problem is the unwillingness of the dog to eat. Foul breath is another symptom of infected gums, as well as swelling and discoloration.

Almost every breed Standard describes the bite desired in the breed. Most call for a scissors bite or a level bite. Scissors bite is when the upper teeth fit closely over the lower teeth. A level bite occurs when the upper front teeth and the lower front teeth meet. A few breeds, such as the Shih Tzu and Lhasa Apso, call for an undershot or reverse scissors bite, in which the lower teeth protrude slightly beyond the upper front teeth. In most breeds this is a fault. An overshot mouth is a fault in all breeds and occurs when the upper teeth protrude beyond the lower teeth. You should know the correct bite for your breed and carefully watch the development of the mouth as the dog grows. Overshot mouths often correct themselves as the lower jaws catch up, but undershot mouths seldom correct themselves. If your dog has a bite that is considered a fault in the breed, you will have a hard time finishing its championship. Many owners never look into the mouth until the first time in the ring when the judge goes to examine the dog. Sometimes that becomes a rude awakening.

You can avoid unpleasant surprises and maintain good dental hygiene for your dog by regularly brushing and scraping the teeth as part of its weekly grooming routine.

BATHING

Show dogs are bathed before every show, and during the time they are being prepared to be shown they should be bathed weekly. There are a few exceptions to this. Some of the harsh-coated breeds, such as some of the Terrier breeds and Working dogs, are not bathed just before they are shown because shampoo tends to soften the coats. However, their leg furnishings are bathed weekly and just prior to every show.

It is easier to scissor and trim a clean dog. The hair will not break as readily, the grooming tools will last longer and the result of your efforts will look better if you work on a freshly bathed animal. The coat grows faster and thicker when the skin is clean, so bathing is a necessary procedure for good health.

You can introduce a young puppy to being bathed providing that you do it in a warm place and dry the puppy thoroughly immediately afterwards. Puppies must become accustomed to the feel and the sound of an electric dryer. Some do not mind them, but others really dislike them. Whether the sound of the motor or the blower

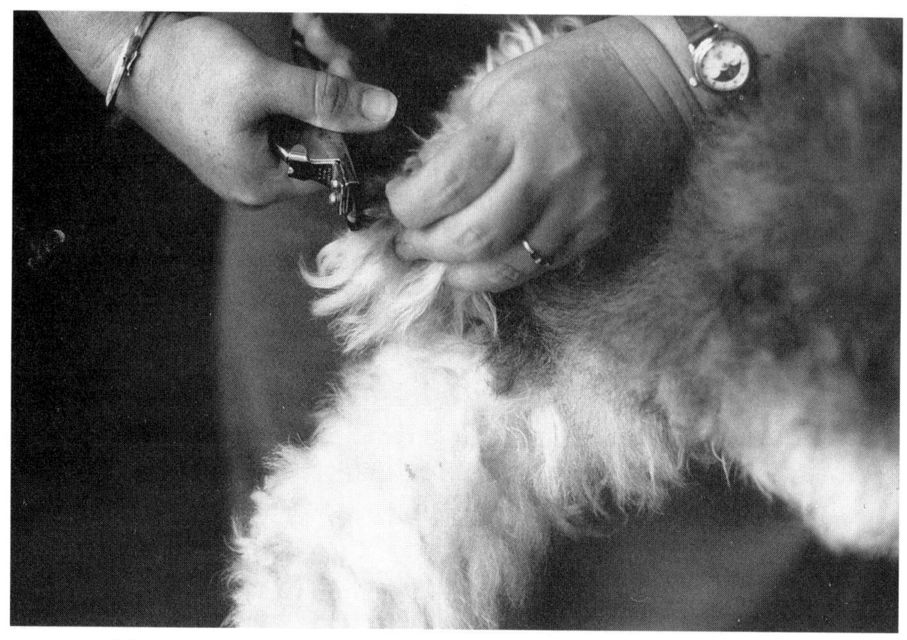

Cutting the nail with a guillotine clipper, take care not to cut into the quick.

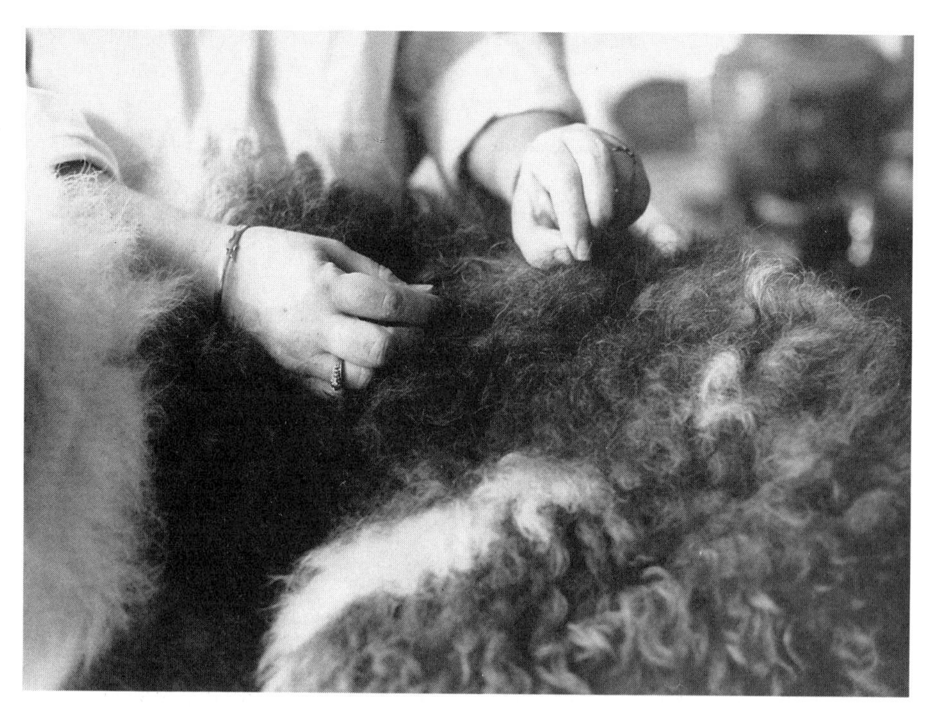

Separate mats with the fingers. . .

. . . then brush the coat to remove dead hair.

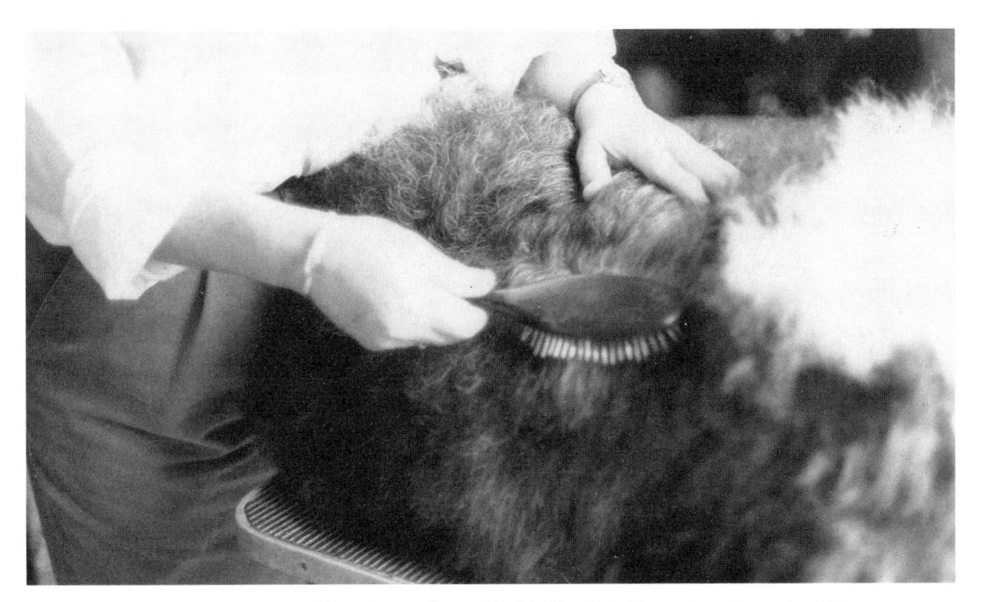

Always brush long coated breeds, such as this Old English Sheepdog, from the skin out.

itself disturbs them is hard to determine. Every show dog should be conditioned to the use of the dryer because it saves hours of towel rubbing and brushing. You can experiment with a dog who fights the dryer by putting cotton in its ears. If sound is the problem, this should alleviate that discomfort somewhat. Some dogs do not mind being blown dry except on the face. In that instance, use it everywhere else and dry the face by hand. You will have to read your dog to find the best compromise for those few animals who really dislike it.

There are shampoos, rinses and conditioners for every imaginable type of coat and skin. There are medicated shampoos for every type of skin ailment. There are insecticide shampoos to ward off fleas and other parasites. There are shampoos for white coats, black coats, red coats and every highlight in between. You will have to experiment with several before you find the one that seems to suit your purpose. There are coat conditioners for every type of coat—silky, harsh, soft, wiry, and smooth. Here, too, you will have to experiment to find the one that suits your dog and complements the shampoo. Every exhibitor has their own formula for success in growing and maintaining a glowing, healthy coat. Most experienced exhibitors know that it is a combination of feeding, breeding and then conditioning that grows a coat.

Coat grows from the inside out. It will be only as healthy as the dog that carries it, and feeding a proper diet is essential. Genetics also play an important part in coat production. If the sire and dam have luxurious coats, your puppy has a good chance of growing one, too, but if they never grew sufficient coat for the breed, your chances of having a heavily coated dog are slim. Climate also plays a part. Dogs in warm sections of the country will rarely produce the coats that their cousins in the cold areas do. Finally, taking care of the coat as it comes in with proper bathing and brushing will help nature along.

BRUSHING

It may seem obvious at first glance that everyone knows how to brush a dog. This is not true. Most people do not brush their dogs properly. This is especially true of the heavily coated breeds. One often hears an owner say, "I brush my dog every day," but when you go over that dog the hair comes off in your hand, and you can feel matted clumps underneath the surface of the coat.

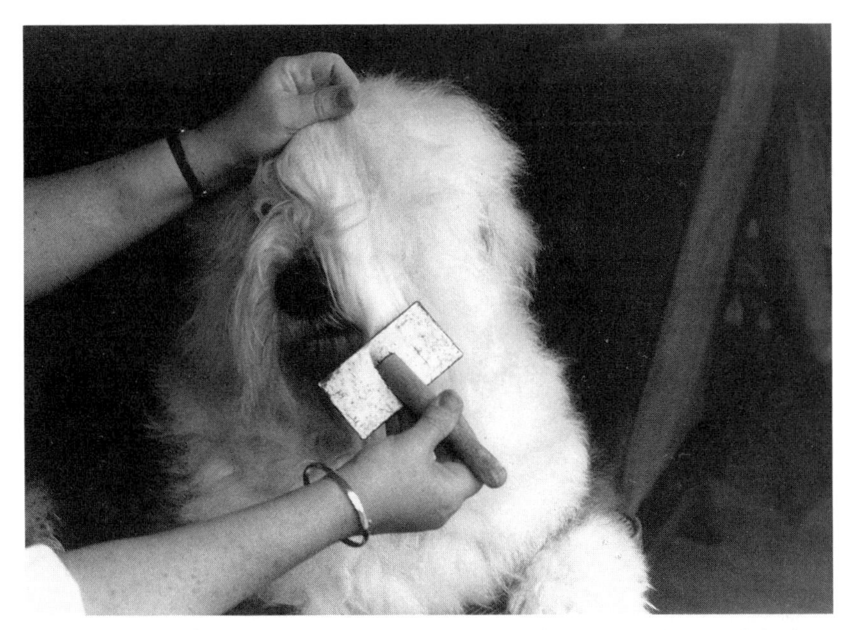

This Old English Sheepdog is being groomed with a soft slicker brush around the face.

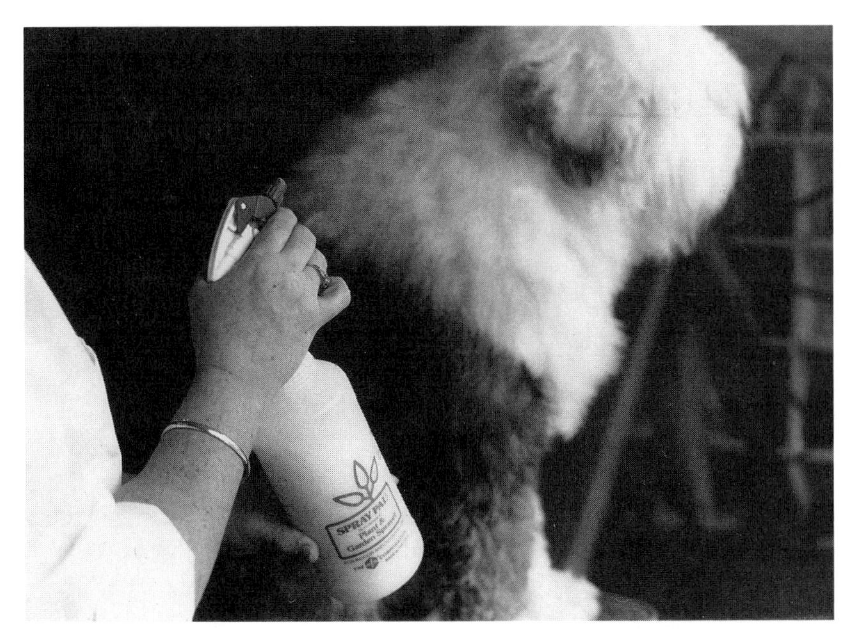

Anti-static spray can be used just before going into the ring.

Coats should be brushed from the skin out. Unless you have a smooth-coated breed, like a Pointer or a Boxer, a pin brush is what you will need to begin. Teach your dog to lie down on its side, and beginning at the head, brush the hair from the skin out to the ends of the coat in small sections. Pay particular attention to those areas under the "arms," on the stomach, behind the ears and where the coat is longest. Once you have completed one side, turn the dog over and do the other. Then stand the dog up, brush the back, under the hind legs and the tail. Each breed has its peculiarities, so you will have to learn the correct technique for your breed. With most breeds you will brush with the grain of the hair. Some breeds, such as the Old English Sheepdog, are back-brushed once they have been thoroughly gone through. There are few instances when you need to use a comb, except to run through the coat once it has been brushed out.

Smooth-coated dogs need brushing, as well. Use a boar bristle brush with the grain of the hair, and follow this with a hound glove, which you run over the body from head to tail. Smooth-coated dogs shed just as much as long-haired breeds, and the best way to get rid of dead hair in these breeds is by bathing, and stripping out the dead coat with a narrow-bladed stripper.

Short-haired breeds have different types of haircoat, just as their longer counterparts do, so each will be treated somewhat differently.

BEYOND THE BRUSH

Grooming a dog for the show ring may be compared to an artist sculpting in clay. You must have a picture in your mind of how the finished dog should look, then you must have the proper tools to accomplish your goal.

In addition to the traditional brushes and combs and, in the case of short coats, gloves, there are many other implements that you will need, according to the breed.

Stripping knives are serrated-edged tools that come with varying sized blades. They are used to take out dead hair and undercoat by raking along the coat with the grain of the hair. The blade lies flat against the coat without digging into the hair, as this will cut the outer coat. Taking out the undercoat helps the shedding process and promotes new growth. It should be done continually as part of the grooming process.

There are dozens of types of scissors, from single-edge thinning

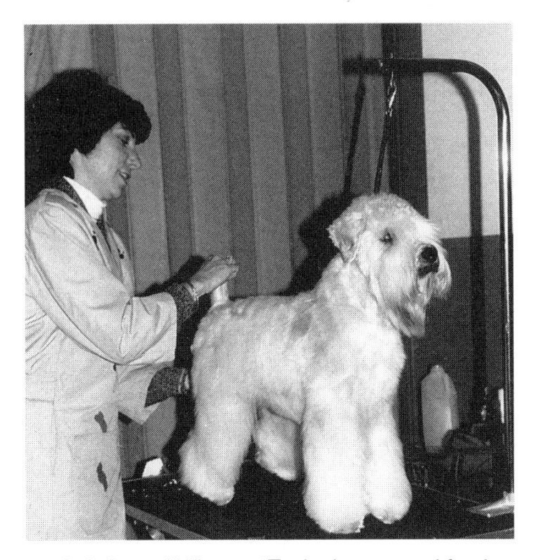

A Soft Coated Wheaten Terrier is prepared for the ring.

This English Springer Spaniel likes a little cool water spray to drink.

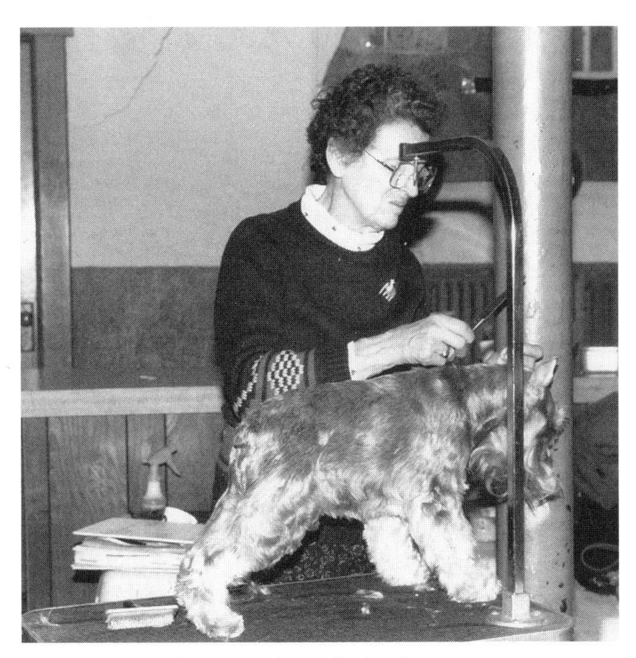

A Miniature Schnauzer is readied in the grooming area.

shears to all manner of straight-edge scissors. The type of implement you use will depend upon the coat length and texture and what you intend to trim. Scissors should be sharp, and the blades should be attended to regularly to maintain their cutting edge. Some thinning shears should be kept sharp and others dull, depending upon their purpose. Scissors should fit your hand and feel comfortable as you work. Otherwise your fingers and hand will become sore.

Fingers are important grooming tools, too. Many dogs are hand stripped, which is a technique needing much practice before you attempt to prepare a dog for the show ring. Hand stripping involves pulling out undercoat and dead hair from the body by grabbing a small amount of hair between the thumb and first finger and pulling, sometimes using a pumice stone to catch the hair. You can tell an experienced groomer by the calluses on his fingers!

In all breeds, grooming for the show ring is quite different from everyday maintenance. It requires patience to learn and to perfect the skills, and a good teacher to impart them to you. If you have ever seen a perfectly groomed Poodle you will appreciate the artistry, time and technique that have gone into its preparation. Good grooming is an essential ingredient of every show dog, and part of the education of every exhibitor.

7

Training the Show Dog

SHOW TRAINING should start from the time the puppy is about ten weeks old and is steady enough on its feet to walk on a lead. It must be emphasized that all early training should be brief and fun for the dog. A few minutes twice a day is all that should be expected. The attention span of puppies is short, and once they lose interest you have lost a vital ingredient for a show dog.

At this early stage you will need your grooming table and a show lead. Use a lead without a separate collar. There are several varieties you can buy, the best selection being found at one of the many vendors who sell supplies at dog shows. The lead should have an adjustable slip collar, tightened sufficiently so the dog cannot back out of it. This is essential if you are practicing in an unfenced area.

To accustom your puppy to the feel of a collar, get a lightweight buckle collar and place it around its neck. The puppy will scratch and buck and attempt to rid itself of the collar, but within a short time other things will occupy its mind and it will forget about it. The next step is to attach a light lead to the collar and allow the puppy to lead you wherever it wants to go. Once it has decided this is no real threat, it is time to gently encourage the puppy to follow you. At this point you can substitute the show lead for the buckle collar and do the same thing. Allow the puppy to lead you, and then you can gently tug on the lead, calling the puppy to you and encouraging it to follow.

As the puppy comes along, a small treat can be given with lots of praise. The puppy should be on your left side, and you should hold your show lead in your left hand. As the puppy gets used to walking or trotting at your side, keep your arm outstretched so the lead falls directly over the puppy's neck. The puppy's head should be just ahead of your leg so it is moving along at your pace without lagging behind you or forging ahead of you. For some breeds this is the place that the dog should always be shown. In other breeds, such as some of the Sporting and Hound breeds, you will want to teach your dog to gait in front of you at the end of the lead. However, this is a sophisticated technique that should only be done with a dog that is totally reliable and experienced.

The novice handler should always aim to control his dog through the use of the lead while it is gaiting.

GAITING PATTERNS

There are five basic gaiting patterns you will need to know and practice with your dog before you show.

Gaiting in a circle is the one routine that every judge uses, no matter how large or small the class. It is the first thing you will do after the judge has checked in the class. With your dog on the left side, mark out a section about the size of the average ring (about 40 × 50 feet) and trot slowly around in a circle within that circumference. Do not allow the dog to sniff the ground or to wind around your ankles. Maintain control through the lead, encouraging the puppy to trot along at your side. Part of being confident in the show ring is to know where you are walking, and it is useful to practice the patterns you may need so you are not taken unawares.

Once you have gotten your puppy so it will go along with you in a circle, it is helpful to ask a friend to bring along a dog to practice. In the show ring you will have someone in front of you and in back of you, causing major distractions for your dog. You don't want your dog to lunge ahead or to twist into a pretzel to see the dog in back of it. Practice is the only way to overcome those temptations. The

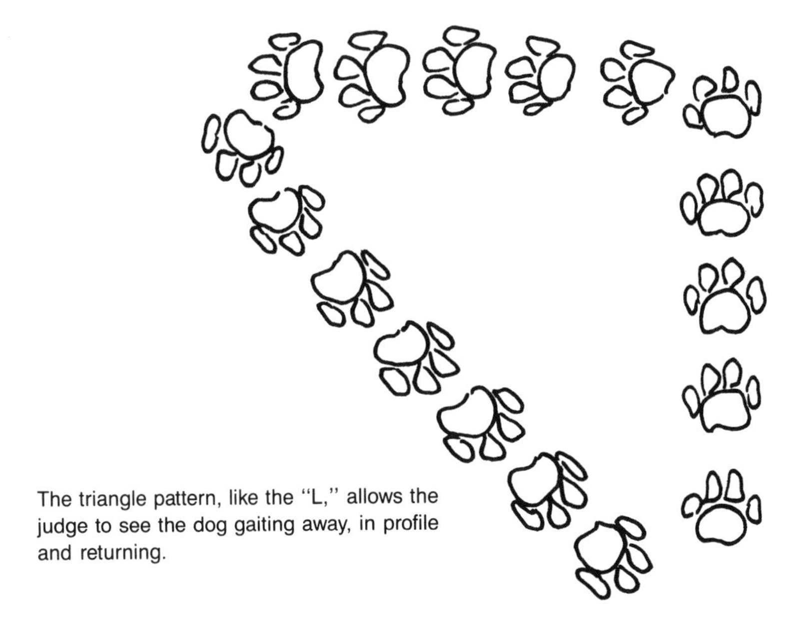

The triangle pattern, like the "L," allows the judge to see the dog gaiting away, in profile and returning.

A straight down and back pattern.

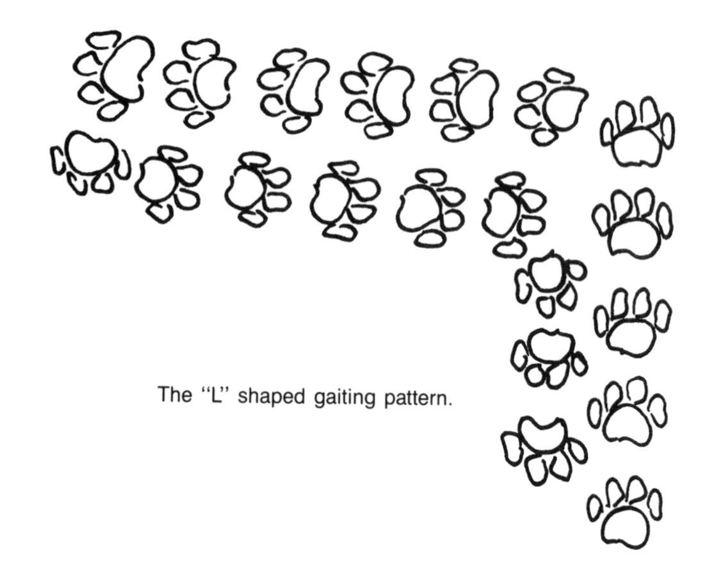

The "L" shaped gaiting pattern.

Gaiting around the ring in a circle, so that the judge may see lateral movement.

dog has to learn to pay attention to you and to follow your lead, no matter what occurs around it. Inconsiderate handlers sometimes allow their dogs to run up on the dog in front of them, and your dog must remain steady during those unsettling circumstances. The only way to condition your dog to ignore this is to practice in a class or with other people willing to help.

Judges have their preferences for seeing dogs gait individually. They may ask you to make a triangle. With the dog on your left side you gait away from the judge to the end of the ring, across the far side of the ring and back on a diagonal to the judge, stopping about five feet in front of him.

Another favorite gaiting pattern is to take the dog straight down to the end of the ring and back to the judge.

A third, less popular pattern is the L. The judge will ask you to take the dog down to the end of the ring, across the far side of the ring, back across the ring and return to the judge. This is a cumbersome pattern, but one you should practice in case it ever comes up.

Sometimes you will find it necessary to change hands while you are gaiting your dog. This is a famous way to thoroughly confuse yourself and your dog unless you know it perfectly ahead of time. You may wish to change hands if you have to do the L, in order for the dog to be between you and the judge. Otherwise the judge will be unable to see the dog. You must change hands with the dog in front of you so it ends up gaiting on your right side. Sometimes a dog will lean into you, and gaiting on the right side will help break this habit. Also, if there is a great deal of distraction at ringside you might want to gait your dog back to the judge so it is on the inside with your body acting as a shield. Changing hands is complicated and awkward and requires a great deal of practice. It is not something you will want to do with a young puppy that is just learning to trot at an even pace.

As your dog grows and matures, it will develop a stride to match its structure. You must observe your dog to determine how fast it should go to look its best. Dog shows are not races, although some handlers feel that the faster the dog goes, no matter what the breed, the better it looks. This is not so, although the speed demons may feel the judge can't see faults of gait or structure if the dog is running the four-minute mile. If the dog is built correctly and has not had an opportunity to develop bad habits of gait, it will look best trotting at a moderate speed.

This Samoyed gaits away from the judge. . .

across the ring. . .

and returns to the judge.

The handler allows the dog to show itself.

Watch your dog as it trots freely in your yard. Ask a friend to gait the dog for you, so you can see what the judge sees.

As the puppy matures and becomes accustomed to the slip lead, you may want to try other types of leads. There are choke collars of various types, and if your dog is difficult to control, you may want to use one of these. Whatever lead and collar you use, keep it simple. Some dogs are examined with collars off, and if yours is one of those breeds, you don't want to be fussing with an intricate arrangement while the judge is waiting. If you are showing your puppy, it is acceptable in all breeds to leave the collar on, so you don't end up chasing your dog as it exits the ring!

STACKING

There are two basic components to showing a dog. One is gaiting; the other is stacking. When you are training a young dog, never do the two things together. Practice gaiting at a different time than you practice stacking. Once the dog has learned both gaiting and stacking, you can put the two lessons together in practice.

If you have one of the "table breeds"—that is, one that is examined on the table instead of on the ground—you must practice stacking your puppy a few minutes every day on the grooming table. Set up a mirror in the room where you will be doing this so you can see what the judge sees when he examines your dog. Set the dog up at one end of the table closest to where the judge will be examining the head. Set the front feet, and then, still holding the dog by the head, set the back feet with the hocks perpendicular to the ground. Practice this several times during a session. When the puppy has the idea of what is expected, ask a friend or family member to approach the dog as if he or she were the judge.

Both "table dogs" and those examined entirely on the ground must be trained to stack on the ground on all types of surfaces. Show venues vary from putting-green smooth grass to rutted hayfields, and from rubber matting to slippery concrete. Whenever possible practice stacking on a variety of surfaces so that your dog is not afraid when he encounters unfamiliar footing.

How you control the head of the dog will determine how well you can control the whole dog. By moving the head in one direction or another you will change the dog's center of gravity. You can make it move its feet, stretch its neck, and, in effect, mold it into a different

An English Setter stacked on the table.

An English Setter stacked on the ground for the judge.

appearance by controlling the head. As you stack it in front of your practice mirror, try different stances so you can see how it looks best. Dog shows are in some degree illusion, and it is up to clever handlers to make their dogs appear to be the very epitome of their breeds.

BAIT

Getting and keeping the dog's attention is an important ingredient in showing your dog. One can see exhibitors in the ring with all sorts of enticements to make the dog appear alert and interested. Squeaky toys are a favorite, and in some rings the sound of latex creatures being squeezed in pockets is quite obvious. Some dogs love tennis balls, and a good handler knows just when to produce a favorite ball to get the dog's ears up just as the judge looks their way. One famous dog loved hot dogs, and his handler was not above carrying a piece of the greasy sausage in his pocket. At Westminster a Group-winning Poodle was seen carrying his favorite toy in his mouth as he gaited around the ring.

Customs about baiting vary among the breeds and also among the judges. Doberman Pinscher rings are a sea of baked liver because the dogs have been taught to focus on that to look attentive. Handlers toss the liver to get the dog to focus away from them and toward the judge. That technique is called free baiting.

Most judges do not mind exhibitors baiting their dogs, but there are some who abhor it. A few will not consider a dog if the handler is baiting it to get attention. You should find out ahead of time by watching the classes before yours or asking other exhibitors about the judge's preference.

Baiting is a skill that can be used effectively to teach your dog to focus, but it should not be used in place of a meal! One tiny piece of dried liver is all you should need to take into the ring. You should practice baiting at home before going into the ring. The bait should be shown to the dog only when you want it to stand still and look up at the judge. It should not be used while you are gaiting because the dog will become so distracted by the idea of the bait that it may twist around to get into your pocket, throwing itself totally off stride.

Bait is not a reward. It is an attention-getter. When you bait your dog, hold the liver in front of its face, but not so close as to make it lean backwards. Do not wave your arm up and down or twirl around like a windmill. When you have its focus where you want it,

This handler is baiting a Standard Poodle puppy for the judge.

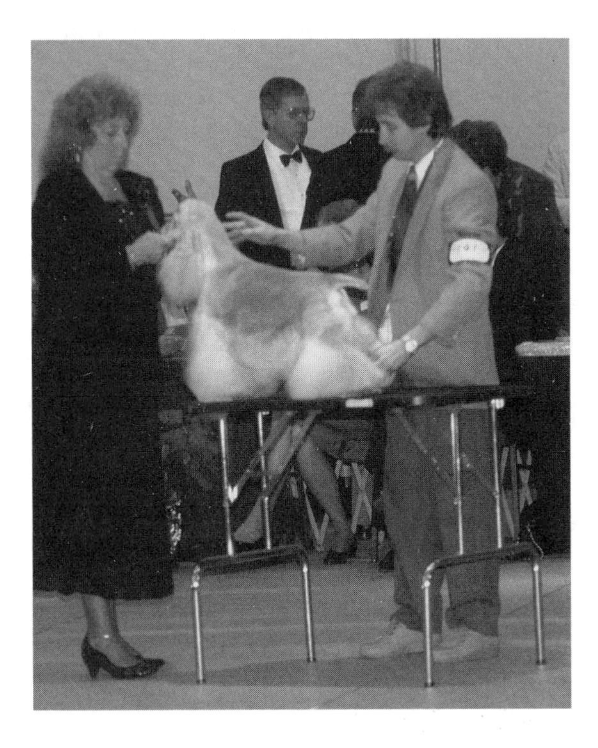

A Cocker Spaniel is examined on the table.

hold your hand still. If you have a large dog, hold your hands between your waist and your chest. If you have a small dog, bend down until you are holding the bait level with the position you want the dog's head to be.

Occasionally you may wish to focus the dog's attention toward the judge and away from you. You may then pretend to throw the bait ahead of you, facing the dog in the direction you wish it to look. You can practice this at home by teaching the dog to retrieve a ball or stick. Keep the dog at your side as you throw out the ball so it can see where the ball is thrown. Send the dog to fetch the ball, and when it retrieves give lots of praise. The basic retrieve is the foundation for many other exercises in obedience, but it makes baiting into a game for the show dog.

Do not use bait as a tool in the show ring if you feel awkward about it. You must be very familiar with the routines of stacking and gaiting quickly and smoothly before you should attempt to do anything else with your hands. There are some dogs who simply are not interested in bait. For those, fiddling with it is useless.

You can use anything as an attention-getter. It can be birds flying overhead, or a dog in another ring, for instance. Do not be afraid to let your dog focus on whatever catches his eye, because that look of interest and vitality reflects in its whole body attitude. Do not, however, allow it to distract another dog in the ring or block the judge's view of another dog. This is done sometimes, but is impolite and unsportsmanlike.

TRAINING THE GROWING DOG

As you practice with your puppy, it will go through several stages, both mentally and physically. Puppies are like children. Sometimes their bodies mature before their minds. This seems to be especially true of the large breeds. You may expect more of them than they are mentally able to give, because they are still babies, even though they may tip the scales at eighty pounds. Growing dogs often go through phases where they are so awkward they can barely maneuver their legs in the same direction. This is usually the time, at about four to nine months, that they are teething. This is a good time to do nothing.

When puppies teethe, their mouths are sore, and putting a lead around their necks is uncomfortable. Leave them alone during these months. Do not consider showing them or fussing with them at all, except for basic maintenance. If you have taught showing procedures of gaiting and stacking at an earlier age, they will remember it and be quite willing to go through it all after their growing pains have ceased.

Many dogs go through a personality change at nine or ten months. They may become fearful of strange places and people. If they have been well socialized as babies, this phase should pass. During this growing period, don't force them into situations in which they are uncomfortable. One caveat to this, of course, is the possibility that you have a dog who is genuinely shy, and this trait will manifest itself as the dog gets older. If this is the case, you may have a serious problem in showing the dog, and you will have to evaluate whether or not it should be shown as a representative of its breed.

Growing dogs will experience structural changes, and often some of the larger breeds will begin to demonstrate some of the problems common to them. Hip dysplasia is one genetic disease that may cause lameness in young dogs. It is characterized by laxity in the hip joints, which eventually leads to changes in the bones of the hip, causing pain and arthritis. The first signs of hip dysplasia are often a bunny-hopping gait, difficulty in getting up from a resting position, discomfort in sitting or standing for long periods. If your dog evidences any of these symptoms it should be X-rayed, because that is the only way to diagnose hip dysplasia.

While the dog is in any pain, you are not going to show it, because a lame dog will be excused from the ring by the judge. But you also have a long-range decision to make. Even though the dog may appear to get better, if he has been diagnosed dysplastic, should he be shown at all? Hip dysplasia is an inheritable trait, and it will progress as the dog gets older. For those reasons you may have to reconsider this dog's show career.

There are other growth diseases that affect young dogs. However, with rest and care they usually outgrow them without permanent damage. Osteochondrosis affects the cartilage in the joints. Panosteitis is a spontaneous, self-limiting disease of the long bones in large breeds. Hypertrophic Osteodystrophy (HOD) is a disease affecting the growth plates in large breeds, characterized by pain and fever from three to seven months of age. There are also genetic bone diseases, such as dwarfism in Alaskan Malamutes, and craniomandibular osteopathy, which is seen in West Highland White Terriers, Cairn Terriers, Boxers, Labrador Retrievers, Rottweilers and Doberman Pinschers. This is a malformation of the jaws and mouth for which there is no cure.

There are many genetic diseases afflicting different breeds, and you should become familiar with those associated with your breed. By knowing the possibilities you will be able to pick up on any abnormalities at an early age, and also consider the consequences of breeding that animal later in life.

All through its growth period you should be evaluating your puppy. By comparing it to others in its breed, you can decide whether you really have a good show potential, and whether you wish to pursue a show career for this dog. There are those within the breed who will help you, but your own powers of observation should be the final determinant.

COMMUNICATING WITH YOUR DOG

The most successful show dogs become a team with their handlers, having learned to respect and to do whatever it takes to please them. They receive their cues from you, and they sense when you are pleased or worried, fearful or anxious. Their attitudes will reflect your frame of mind, whether or not you verbalize your anxieties. You must learn to project confidence to your dog. It must believe that it is doing well and that you are proud of it. Experienced show dogs know when they have done something right—they may not know that they have won a huge class, or a Group or Best in Show—but they certainly know that you are happy and that they have caused your jubilation.

Show dogs may be born with correct conformation, but the "look-at-me-I'm-a-star" attitude is made. Breeders look for the most outgoing puppy in the litter as the one who has the temperament to be a good show dog. However, this is not always the case. An innate sense of security is as important to a show dog as the puppy's clamoring for attention. Some of the most famous show dogs have been those who possessed a dominant attitude without a frenetic personality. Among them are dogs who appear to be the essence of laziness, until the show lead goes around their necks and they enter the ring. At that moment one can see them transformed into actors on a stage.

Given a puppy with a stable, outgoing temperament, an owner can develop those traits into the personality needed to be a show dog.

An English Springer Spaniel stacked after a big win.

Socialization is perhaps the most important ingredient. It is essential to get the puppy out into different situations while it is still in its formative months. A puppy who never sees the outside of its kennel run or yard until it goes to its first show will have a difficult time making the adjustment from house pet to show dog. As soon as the puppy has had all its shots, take it out to the shopping center, to the school playground, walking on the street, anyplace where it will be exposed to strange people, noises and sights. While you are walking it in public, reassure and praise it. Allow people to come up to it so it gets used to a stranger's touch. By exposing the puppy to different circumstances, it will not be fearful when the judge approaches it in the ring. All the while, you are building its confidence and telling it how great it is. The dog may not understand your words, but it will understand your tone of voice and body language.

Dogs are very observant. Owners often do not realize that they are signaling to their dogs by the way they stand, move their hands and feet, twist or jerk the lead. You must convey your message to the dog, not only verbally, but through your actions. If you are nervous, that emotion will travel right down the lead to your dog, and it will react. If you want your dog to be confident, alert, outgoing and cheerful, you must pretend to be all those things, even if your heart is in your shoes. The "power of positive thinking" was never more appropriate than in the making of the show dog.

THE PSYCHOLOGY OF WINNING

Physical coordination and a certain amount of agility are important in the presentation of a show dog. Obviously, large breeds will require more stamina and fitness than Toy breeds, but everyone who shows a dog must be at least able to get around a show ring without falling down!

Mental agility is as important as physical fitness in the show ring. You must be mentally prepared to go into competition, and this training takes as much time and intellectual discipline as the physical exercise you give yourself and your dog.

To begin with the basics, while you are practicing your stack, gait and bait routines, think about how your dog looks best, how you will hold the lead, when you will take it off, under what circumstances you will change hands. In other words, while you are practicing, you should mentally prepare for any circumstance you might encounter in the ring. These things should be as much a part of your daily practice as the physical motions. If you can picture in your mind the possible contingencies, you can, without using the dog, establish a mind-set that will carry over into the show ring.

Your attitude is important to success. You must have confidence in your dog and in yourself, and you can use simple psychological techniques to help you achieve a positive mental picture. You can build your own self-confidence by eliminating all the extraneous factors that might hinder you and concentrate instead on the best features of your dog. For instance, do not worry about the competition. Let the competition worry about you. Relax by slowing down your actions so you are not concerned about how fast the judge is coming toward you. The half second longer that it takes you to stack the dog properly may make the difference between win and lose.

Concentrate! Focus all your attention on your dog and on the judge. Let others chat at ringside or amongst one another. Until you are thoroughly familiar with every aspect of the show ring you should stick to the business at hand.

Nothing succeeds like success. If you have won with your dog, think about that as you go into the next show. Be positive and your attitude will be projected into your actions. Think about winning that class, or that Breed, Group or Best in Show.

Mental preparedness is the basis for success in all sports, from team sports like football to individual sports such as tennis or golf. How often one hears the loser of a tennis match say, "I lost my concentration." It is as taxing to be mentally disciplined as it is to be physically fit. The two go together, but in the world of dog shows, the mental attitude is even more important than the physical attributes of being able to run the triangle or the circle.

The psychology of winning has become a popular subject among team managers of the major sports. Some professional teams hire psychologists to motivate players into thinking positively about winning the next game. You can do the same by combining the physical skills you have learned in presenting your dog with the mental attitude to win.

The combination of those two attitudes will give you the winning edge.

Ch. Finlair Tiger of Stone Ridge and handler Bob La Rouech reap the rewards of being well prepared for the ring.

8

Preparing for the Show Ring

YOU MAY DECIDE to introduce yourself and your puppy to its show career by attending show handling classes. These are usually sponsored by either all-breed or specialty clubs in the community. You can find out the names of the clubs in your area by contacting the American Kennel Club, 51 Madison Avenue, New York, NY 10010. This fount-of-all-information organization can also put you in touch with the names of show superintendents so you can discover when shows will be coming to your region. The American Kennel Club also publishes, through its monthly publication, *The Gazette,* a list of all shows held throughout the United States during the year.

Between the American Kennel Club and your local club, either all-breed or specialty, you should be able to learn when and where shows and matches will be held so you can get started.

Tack boxes come in various sizes.

A private exercise pen allows these Pugs to eye a Great Dane from a safe distance.

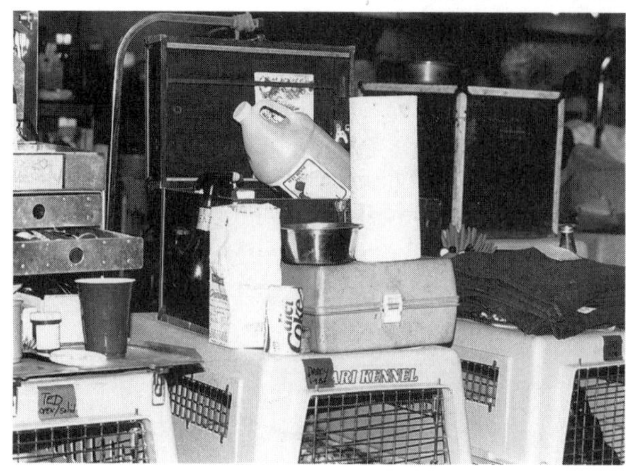

Dog show people are great "schleppers."

MATCH SHOWS

There is no absolutely best time to begin to show a puppy. There are match shows for puppies as young as three months. These events are generally casual and attract people who want to bring their youngsters out to practice. You can enter on the day of the show, and there you will find other novice handlers with inexperienced dogs.

People ordinarily do not attend matches for the opinion of the judge as much as to work on their ring routines. Often judges at match shows are practicing their skills, too. Aficionados usually do not put much credit on winning at matches, although it is always better to win than to lose at any event! Matches are a good place to start a show career because of the low-key atmosphere. No one cares if you or your puppy goofs up.

Specialty matches, those run by the local breed club for your breed, are another good way to be introduced to the show ring. There you will be able to evaluate your puppy against others of its kind.

POINT SHOWS

After you have attended a few matches and have learned the basic techniques of showing your puppy, you will be ready for the real thing. Puppies six months and older are eligible to enter point shows.

These are pre-entered shows, and you can obtain entry forms, which are called premium lists, from the show-giving club, from the Superintendent of the show or through the *AKC Gazette* show listings, which contain blank entry forms. In the Appendix of this book you will find a sample entry form and instructions for filling one out.

Entries must include the dog's registered name and number. If for some reason you were not given a registration certificate, or a registration form for you to send to the American Kennel Club when you purchased your puppy, you must get this matter taken care of first. The dog's entire record of show wins is predicated on its registration number, so this is as important to its career as your Social Security number is to you. In addition, if you ever want to breed the dog, you will need this number to register the puppies.

Try to start your show career in a small show. Enter in the Puppy class. In most breeds at small shows there are very few in competition in the Puppy classes. Entry fees are high, so many exhibitors prefer to wait until their dog is mature and show it when they have a better chance to win the points. However, just because you will have little competition in your class, you will have a good opportunity to practice your skills and discover exactly what the judges are up to. If you are the only one in your class, you will have to return to compete for Winners Dog or Winners Bitch, and then you will have other dogs in the ring with you. Puppies are always placed at the end of the line in the Winners class.

In some of the smaller and faster-maturing breeds it is entirely possible to win from the Puppy class, and even in some of the larger breeds a flyer occasionally appears to take the points over the older dogs.

Some people elect to show in the Puppy class only at Specialty shows or supported shows where there are many entries because they feel that only winning in large competition means anything.

Specialty shows are those held by the local breed club or the national breed club. The number of local Specialties depends entirely on how many local breed clubs there are. The number varies depending on the breed. A few breeds have as many as sixty local clubs, whereas the majority have far fewer. All breed clubs have one National Specialty show during the course of the year, although a few clubs have two. Usually the site of the National Specialty rotates around the country. Clubs have different ways of organizing their National Specialties, though in almost all cases the number of entries is large for the breed and the show is considered a showcase of the best dogs in the country. Even if you do not enter a National Specialty when you are just starting, it is worthwhile to attend and watch. Often there are symposia and other interesting and enjoyable events accompanying a National, and a newcomer can learn a great deal just by being there.

9

Plan, Pack, Go!

DOG SHOW PEOPLE are the world's greatest "schleppers." If you ask them what to take to a show, they will tell you "everything," and when you see them unloading their cars and vans at a show, you can see that they are not exaggerating. What comes out of the typical show goer's vehicle is reminiscent of the clown's car at the circus. You wonder how they crammed it all in to get there.

WHAT TO TAKE TO A DOG SHOW

What you take in part depends upon whether it is an outdoor show or an indoor show.

Take the outdoor shows first. You will bring a chair to sit on and some sort of sunshade for you and for your dog. A sunshade can be as simple as an umbrella or as elaborate as a tarpaulin that you erect at your spot or attach to your car with clips. There are some interesting products available at dog show concessions. One is a mesh sunscreen that blocks out the rays and keeps the area relatively comfortable. The other is a cloth that is silver on one side to reflect the sun and dark on the other to absorb the heat in the event that it is cold outside. This goes over the windshield or is hung on the

A sturdy carrier particularly good in warm weather and approved for airline travel.

sides of the car with metal clips, which you can buy at the same time.

If it is summer, you will bring ice in a thermos cooler and wet down towels, just in case it gets very hot. You will want to bring something to eat and drink, since food at dog shows is notoriously bad. That goes in the cooler with the ice. Wear clothing in layers, since it is often cool in the morning and hot midday. Always keep raingear and boots in the car, because sudden showers are guaranteed at outdoor shows!

Some exhibitors prefer to use their own exercise pens, because it is much more sanitary than to use the public exercise areas provided by the show-giving club. Some clubs do not permit private ex pens, but these are mostly indoor shows. Exercise pens come in sections. You can buy them welded together or separately. They are available in different heights, depending on your breed. Some have sections with gates on them, while others do not. Prices vary according to the manufacturer and the size. They are on display at most supply concessions at shows. Unless you also buy a top for your ex pen, it is not a good idea to leave a dog alone in one. Even the smallest or most docile dog can climb or jump out if sufficiently motivated. Along with the ex pen, you must have pooper scoopers to clean up after the dog. These are also available where you buy the pen.

Bug repellent is useful to carry to outdoor shows, as is hydrocortisone to put on bee stings. Antihistamine comes in handy occasionally if you or your dog are at the business end of a bee or wasp.

When you are packing for an indoor show, you should take all of the same equipment as for an outdoor, with the possible exception of the sunshade and the ex pen. Since some indoor shows get very hot, carry the ice and the towels for wetting down an overheated dog, though this is rare. Some shows, though held indoors, have outside areas where ex pens are permitted, so you should bring it along in case you are able to use it.

Common to all shows are the paraphernalia deemed absolutely necessary by any seasoned fancier. First, the crate. It matters not what kind of crate you prefer to carry your dog, it is an essential component for peace of mind and to ward off exhaustion. Crates come in any size, from tiny for Toy dogs, to huge for the giant breeds. You can buy them made of wire, aluminum, wood or fiberglass. If you travel by air, you will need a fiberglass or aluminum crate. One word of caution about both. They get very hot and should really not be used at outdoor shows in the summer. If a large crate is necessary for your breed, you should purchase a dolly to pull it. Some grooming tables come with wheels, so that you get a dolly and a table together.

Crates make the life of show dog and exhibitor much easier. They provide a safe travel compartment in the car and a refuge for the dog to relax in while at the shows. A show dog should not spend half the day waiting to go into the ring being walked around the show grounds, getting dirty on the grass or floor, or exhausted lunging at other dogs. It should be kept quiet in its crate until it is time to be exercised and groomed before its appearance in the ring.

Crate training, incidentally, is an essential part of any show dog's life. They spend a great deal of time in their crates, particularly if you are going to two or three shows in a row and are traveling between them. Even if you stay at the same place for a series of shows, called a circuit, the dog must be content to be confined to a crate for long periods of time. Dogs in motels should always be crated and never left alone outside of their crates in the room. Should someone enter the room where a dog is left loose, it could escape out the door and be gone. A dog left alone in a strange place could become fearful and do considerable damage to the furnishings. In fact, many such occurrences have caused a large number of motels to refuse to accept dogs in the rooms at all. Show goers have found themselves locked out of most hotels and motels throughout the country because of the inconsiderate actions of a few.

The use of a crate at home makes housetraining easy. The puppy learns to associate the crate as its home, and will not soil its own bed. When you are unable to be with the puppy, you can put it in its crate and it will be satisfied to rest until you are able to take it out to play and exercise. Never abuse a crate, however, by leaving a puppy, or an adult dog, in one for hours at a time. A crate is a convenience, but it should not be used as a substitute for adequate facilities to house an animal if an owner must be away at work.

To protect your dog and protect the rights of others, buy and use a crate. They are available at almost every dog supply concession at shows, through catalogs and at some pet shops. They vary in price depending upon the make, material and size. Shop around to get the one that best fits your needs.

A grooming table is the next heavy item you will need at a show. You can use the same table as the one you've been using at home for grooming and stacking, providing it has collapsible legs, of course. A grooming arm is useful to help keep the dog on the table, although you will never leave it alone!

Exhibitors have many ways of telling others about their hobby.

Grooming tools are essential, and you can either buy a tack box from a show concessionaire or you can devise your own. Tack boxes come in wood or aluminum in various sizes and varying prices. Some people use such diverse things as overnight luggage or fishing tackle boxes. Whatever fits your needs and is portable can be used, and what you put into it will depend upon your breed. Basic grooming tools, leads, collars, bait, pills for sudden diarrhea or bee stings, a pen, some small change for a soft drink, rubber bands for fastening on your armband, a spray bottle with water to mist the dog down if it is warm, coat dressing, squeaky toys: these are some of the things you will find in almost any grooming box. What you add or leave out is up to you. It is considered acceptable to borrow a comb, a scissors or a small piece of liver occasionally. It is not proper to come week after week without your own equipment, including the grooming and showing aids and the table.

Bring the water, the water bowl and your own picnic, if you can't stand the thought of another hot dog or weak coffee. Although ringside is usually very crowded at indoor shows, you may want to sit by your crate when you are not in the ring, so bring a folding chair with your name on it.

EQUIPMENT FOR THE CAR

When you start going to shows, you will find yourself doing a great deal more traveling than you ever thought possible. One of the nice things about dog shows is that you get to visit places you would never see without an incentive such as this. Not all shows are located in the world's finest tourist meccas, but driving to them can provide the whole family with new sights and memories of interesting people and places.

Dog shows are often held in out-of-the-way locations, so you will want to be sure your car is functioning well. You will need four good tires and a spare, plus battery cables and a tool kit so you, or some handy person, can perform simple remedies when you are out in a pasture far from any telephone or service station.

A CB or a car phone is a great asset in an emergency. CBs are particularly useful if you get lost and want local information to direct you to your destination.

You should always carry a blanket, a flashlight and emergency flares. Dog people are on the road early in the morning and often late at night, when safety measures are most important. A map or road atlas of the states you'll be driving through should be included. Most premium lists contain directions to the show, but often they are vague, and you will have to navigate unfamiliar territory. Also, it is a good idea to look at a map the night before and estimate how long it will take you to drive to the show. You don't want to cut yourself short and find out that you miscalculated and missed your class, or that you cut the minutes so close you will have no time to prepare yourself and your dog properly.

There is often a limited access to a show site, and traffic tends to back up as people unload their gear before driving away to a parking lot. Extra time must be left for that. The early birds at a show, especially an outdoor show, will get the parking places closest to the rings, and you will find that those who attend shows every week make sure to arrive at their destinations early in the morning to claim the coveted spots.

One of the considerations in parking is the proximity of motor homes. Many clubs assign motor homes to a designated area, but some do not. If you are not traveling in a motor home or pulling a trailor, try to park elsewhere. Motor homes are equipped with generators that exhaust noxious fumes and are very noisy when they are running. All motor homes carry propane tanks, which if not properly maintained can explode, destroying not only the motor home itself, but anything nearby. There have been stories of motor homes catching fire due to leaking propane, demolishing themselves and other vehicles.

HAZARDS OF THE SHOW RING

Dogs shows are held year round, in all sorts of weather, under all kinds of conditions. Dog show exhibitors are a hardy lot, but being prepared for every eventuality will make your experiences bearable, if not pleasant, all the time. Even the terrible experiences make good stories later on.

There are famous tales of tornadoes blowing through the tents, of rain so heavy that the toy dogs were gaited on tables set end to end, of mud so deep that it took heavy tractors to pull the cars out. Dog fanciers love to outdo each other with the best "were you there when . . ." stories.

The most important thing to remember at a show is the welfare

Spectators bring chairs to ringside.

A sun parasol can be handy.

of your dog. When you arrive, try to find a place where you are not crowded in the midst of a handler with a large number of crates and grooming tables and dogs to get ready for the ring. If you plan to unload under the grooming tent at an outdoor show, look for a spot at the end of the tent where you will have access to your ex pen and greater circulation of air. Before you unload, locate your ring and set up under the tent closest to it. This way you will not have far to walk if the weather is bad, and you will be near your dog if you wish to watch the judging at ringside before your turn to go in. You can keep an eye on the dog and your possessions without having to go halfway across the field.

If you decide to park and leave the dog in its crate in the car instead of unloading, try to find a tree to park under for shade. You'll have to get there very early in the morning to accomplish this. Never, ever leave a dog in a car unless it is confined to a crate so you can open all the windows all the way. Heatstroke is one of the most serious dangers at shows, and it is surprising how many people who should know better leave their dogs in cars for hours at a time. Even if you park in the shade, remember that the earth moves around the sun, and your shady place in the morning can quickly become the sunny spot by noon. Many exhibitors seem to forget Galileo's theories when they go to shows. Even with an ideal spot, always check on your dog frequently. Sometimes dogs become frightened and anxious if they are left, particularly young and inexperienced dogs. They can work themselves up into a frantic state in a short time if left alone. Sometimes exhibitors forget that they are there for the dogs and not for a social gathering.

Heat is a danger in the summer and cold can be equally dangerous in winter. Dogs left in unheated cars, or in drafty buildings, can become chilled and vulnerable to illness. If you must leave your dog in a cold lot, cover the crate with a blanket to keep the draft out and the body heat in. Young and frail dogs, such as some of the Toy breeds, should wear sweaters or be wrapped in blankets to keep out the chill.

Use common sense in walking or carrying your dog through the show grounds. Always keep your dog on a short lead, close to your side, and under complete control. Do not allow it to lunge at other dogs or to stray out to the end of the lead. It can become entangled in another dog's lead, or it can invite attack by a passing dog. Small dogs should always be carried through crowded areas. They can be stepped upon or attacked before you can react. Large dogs some-

Precious Cargo

Fanciers enjoy letting you know "what's on board."

times consider the tiny ones as prey, something to be picked up and shaken. That is the end of your story. Be aware and stay alert when taking your dog through the show areas or standing at ringside.

The more you can shelter your dog from others, the greater the opportunity to avoid some of the intestinal and respiratory illnesses that float around at dog shows. If at all possible, avoid the public ex pens. If that is impossible, because you are at an indoor show or a benched show where dogs are not allowed to leave the premises, try to find one that is away from the beaten track. If that, too, is impossible, leave the dog there as short a time as possible. You may have to clean up the pen before you let your dog enter, if the person before you has been inconsiderate. Always clean up after your dog both at indoor and outdoor shows.

Comfortable and sturdy shoes with rubber soles that minimize slipping are a must. Outdoor ring hazards include holes or ruts in the ground into which you can fall, unless you are observant and look at the ring before you enter it to compete. Tent poles that protrude into the ring are another danger. When you are circling the ring, be aware of the posts and try to avoid them. They can give you a nasty bruise on the shin, not to mention tripping you and your dog.

Slippery grass is a hazard about which you cannot do much except pace yourself, especially at the corners where you have to turn in the ring.

Indoor shows have their share of pitfalls, as well. Slippery mats are the most common. Mats sometimes slide out from under you as you gait, or they will bunch up to trip you as you run along. Carpeted floors can be deceptively slippery, also. Be aware of the possibilities and pace yourself according to the conditions of the floor. If you feel yourself falling, try not to land on your dog. Rather than grip the lead tighter, which is a natural reaction, release it, though still holding on to the end, so the dog can get away from you to go to the end of the lead. At indoor shows it is probably safe to let go of the lead. Someone will grab the dog. This may not be wise at an outdoor show, where the dog can elude people and run away. If you know that your dog is not an escape artist, you can drop the lead until you recover your balance.

If you fall while you are gaiting, it is perfectly acceptable to return to the corner just before you took the dive and repeat the pattern. You cannot start all over again from the beginning, however.

If you have a veterinary emergency at a dog show, what to do?

Foul weather gear is a must.

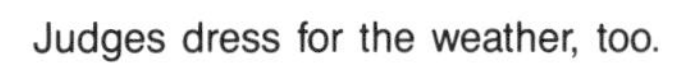

Judges dress for the weather, too.

All clubs are required to list in their premium list the name of a local veterinarian who is either "on call" or present on the grounds. If your dog becomes ill at a show, go at once to the superintendent or show chairman's tent and ask for the veterinarian. If one is at the show, your dog will be attended to immediately. If not, ask for the name of the veterinarian on call. If there is a phone on the grounds, use it to find the location of the clinic before you put the dog into the car and drive off. In the absence of a phone, go to the closest public phone and get directions on your way to the vet.

For people emergencies, large clubs engage the services of the local rescue or first aid squad to stand by on the grounds. Small shows generally do not have that service, but the club is responsible for locating the nearest emergency clinic, to which you will be directed.

With your preparations complete, your entries posted and your confirmation received, you are ready to attend your first show as an exhibitor.

10

Just Before the Show

THE NIGHT BEFORE a show you will have packed all your gear into the car, so you will not be under stress and apt to forget some vital piece of equipment in the morning when you are ready to leave. Exercise your dog before you leave to make certain it will not require a pit stop after you have driven to the end of your street. Organization and a smooth flow of events produce much less stress, both for you and for your dog.

THE ENTRY TICKET

The week prior to the show, you will have received your entry ticket in the mail. This lists the name of the dog, owners, breeders, class entered, registration number and entry number. Check this information to be certain it is correct before you go to the show. If you detect an error, such as the dog being entered in the wrong class, when you arrive at the show you must go to the Superintendent's table at once, or in the case of an independently run show, to the Show Secretary. They will have all the original entries with them and so will be able to check your information against theirs. If they are in error, they will correct the judge's book before the class begins. If you were in error when you sent it in, you may have to forfeit your entry. If it is a matter of an incorrect registration number, or some technical mistake of that nature, it can be rectified and you may proceed to show your dog.

THE JUDGING SCHEDULE

In the same envelope with your entry ticket, which you may have to show at the exhibitor's entrance, there will be a judging schedule. This schedule will show all the breeds in each ring and will list the time each is estimated to be judged. The judging schedule will also often include a diagram of the show grounds, so you can figure out the best place to park or unload near your ring.

No breed can be judged before the time listed in the judging schedule, but if a judge starts at 9:00 A.M., for instance, and has four breeds to judge in the morning, the three following the first breed may not have times listed individually. Therefore, you will have to estimate by the number of dogs listed for each breed in the schedule approximately when your breed will be judged. On the average a judge does twenty-five dogs per hour, so if the first breed at 9:00 A.M. has twenty-five dogs, you can anticipate that the second breed will be ready to go into the ring at about 10:00. If there are absentees, the judge will be through before the hour, and you must be prepared for that. Some judges are very fast and whip through their classes before you can turn around. Many an exhibitor has been caught throwing their entry away because they estimated wrong by a few minutes. Leave yourself enough time to get your dog to the ring comfortably, but no so far in advance as to wear the dog and yourself out standing at ringside. You will be able to estimate times more easily with practice.

SCOPING OUT THE RING

When you have situated yourself at the show, and taken care of any clerical matters (which are rare, incidentally), you should proceed to the ring in which you will be showing your dog. If you get there before any judging starts in the morning, or between breeds being judged in that ring, you are permitted to enter the ring and look around. Walk the perimeter to determine the size of the ring and, in the case of an outdoor show, to see if there is bumpy terrain or potholes you should avoid.

If you are not in time to do these preliminary observations, be sure to arrive at your ring well ahead of your class so you can see other people navigating their way around. If you are the first class, and your judge is judging another breed directly ahead of yours, then watch a few of those classes so you will know what instructions the judge is giving to the exhibitors. That way you can practice your mental stacking and gaiting before you enter the ring.

RING STEWARDS

Each ring is staffed by either one or two ring stewards. These people are there to make sure the correct classes get into the rings quickly, that the judge has a judging book and a pen, that the exhibitors get their numbers and that any trophies and ribbons are ready to be given out after each class is judged. One of their most important duties is to give out armbands (numbers) to every exhibitor. Your entry ticket will show your dog's number, which you should know before you go to the ring steward. However, if you have forgotten your number, it will appear in the catalog that is in each ring. Once you know your number, ask the ring steward for, say, "Puppy Dog Number 5." When you receive your armband, check to be sure the steward has given you the correct number. Slip it on your left arm above the elbow. Fasten it securely with an extra rubber band, which is usually provided at the steward's table. This should all be done well in advance of your dog's ring time.

CATALOGS

Every show is required to provide a catalog listing every exhibitor in every class for each breed. Some catalogs are simple, rather plain, businesslike affairs. Others are quite elaborate, printed on beautiful paper with illustrations. Specialty catalogs are often crammed with ads and are quickly snapped up early in the morning. Some of the top all-breed shows also produce fine catalogs, which over time become collector's items.

It is not essential to purchase a catalog for every show you enter. But you should look at one to be certain your dog is listed correctly, with the name spelled right and numbers correct. In case your dog places in its class, the win will be recorded in the Show Awards section of the *AKC Gazette,* so it should be perfect.

WHAT TO WEAR

We mentioned dressing for the weather in layers and in comfortable shoes. The latter are absolutely essential. Sneakers, any kind of rubber or crepe-soled flat shoes are acceptable. Slippery soles, high heels or sandals are not only inappropriate for the show ring, but are dangerous. Women can wear socks or stockings, depending on the weather. Duck boots are acceptable for both men and women if the grounds are wet or muddy, as is any kind of sturdy, rubber or crepe-soled shoes or sneakers in dry weather or indoors.

Men should always wear jackets and ties, unless it is so hot as to be unbearable. Men can take their cue from the judge. If he is fully attired, you should be, too. Short-sleeved shirts under jackets are acceptable. Rain jackets or down jackets for cold weather are permissible.

Women should wear skirts and blouses, simple dresses or tailored slacks. Flamboyant outfits, miniskirts, low-cut tops or jeans are inappropriate in the show ring. Whatever you wear, it should have pockets. Show goers after a while become so pocket-conscious that even their evening gowns have pockets in them! Bangle jewelry is frowned upon, as it can distract the judge and the dogs in the ring.

Both men and women should dress conservatively so the judge will concentrate on the dog and not on the person behind it. Good handlers do not need to resort to tricks to pull the judge's eye away from the dog and onto themselves.

Clothes should be unobtrusive, but should contrast where possible with the dog. For instance, if you have a black dog, do not wear black because the judge will not be able to see your dog as you stand behind it in the ring. Wear contrasting colors. If you have an Irish Setter, you can wear green to good advantage. And if you have a Dalmatian, do not wear polka dots!

Long, floppy skirts or loud checked pants draw the judge's eye away from the dog. This may be what you want if you have a poor specimen in the ring, but if the idea is for the judge to examine the dog and not your couture, conservative is the operative word. Long skirts also effectively hide small dogs so the judge may never see them at all! Do not wear anything that you will have to fuss with in the ring.

Men should wear slacks with belts that keep their shirttails tucked in. A man should not be dressing himself in the presence of the judge. Hats that fly off, scarves that wave about and obscure your vision should be left in the grooming area. Long hair should be tied back or done up so it does not get in the way of the dog or of your handling. This is true for men and women, and for juniors as well.

At this show, a class of Afghan Hounds waits for the judge's examination.

11

At the Show

DOG SHOWS are made up of four components: the breeder, the dog, the exhibitor and, last but not least, the judge. Who is this person for whose opinion we pay a large amount of money? Who is the person who, by pointing a finger one way or another, can cause such joy, anger, frustration or pain?

THE JUDGES

A judge is a human being, after all, who has elected to transform himself or herself from the ranks of the other three elements into a person whose opinion people will pay an entry fee to seek. Judges all began as breeders and exhibitors, and they must have had several years of experience and a modicum of success as both in order to apply to the American Kennel Club to judge their first breed. Initially, in order to be an approved AKC judge, one must not only be a breeder who has produced champions, one must also have experience as an exhibitor and have been involved in other aspects of the dog fancy.

Judging at matches or in Sweepstakes classes is a requirement to judge at point shows, as is involvement with a club as a steward, a show chairman or show secretary. In addition, prospective judges must pass oral and written tests on the breed they apply for, and in many cases are asked to evaluate a class of dogs and give reasons for their placements before a panel of experts.

Judges usually apply first for the breed with which they are most familiar. Once approved, they may proceed to apply for other breeds, going through the same procedures of testing and evaluation. It takes many years for a judge to be approved for an entire Group. There are fewer than two dozen judges approved for all breeds individually. Judges may apply to judge Best in Show after they have been approved for one Group.

There is often talk at ringside about the competence, honesty and even the birthright of some judges. Most of it should be taken with a grain of salt. If you have never shown to a particular judge before, it is worth a try. The rule of thumb is to give a judge two chances to evaluate your dog. If you have lost twice, it is safe to assume that the judge really does not like your dog and you can save yourself an entry fee the next time that name appears on the panel of a show near you.

Judges who are approved to pass on many breeds and several groups are greatly in demand by clubs, because the club can hire fewer judges. These are not necessarily better judges than those who are approved for only one or two breeds. It merely means they have been at it longer, or are ambitious to amass a lot of breeds to judge.

In almost every breed there are a few judges whose opinion is valued, and to whom people will show even though they may feel that they will not win. On the other hand, there are judges to whom people show just because they know someone will win the points that day, and maybe they will get lucky.

Years ago people showed dogs only to those judges whose opinion they respected. Today shows are more complicated. The win means more than the opinion. Entries are larger, fees are higher and the idea of crowning a champion is more important to most people than whether that dog is truly worthy of the title. Dog shows are a reflection of our society, and judges play their role in the best manner they can. Of the hundreds of judges approved by the AKC, a few are truly dedicated, knowledgeable dog people who can spot a good one in almost any breed. The majority are tradesmen who have learned their job but bring little flair, imagination or that crucial "eye for a dog" that separates them at the top. At the bottom are those who use their judging assignments to reward their friends and exercise their power, or those who are plainly incompetent. Fortunately for the future of the sport, the last category is the smallest.

As you proceed in your show career you will encounter all three types, and eventually you will be able to pick and choose to whom you show your dog.

A file system is useful to keep track of those judges you would like to show to again. It can be done either on a computer or on 3 × 5 cards, listing the judge, the show, the dog you entered, your placement and any comments you have about the judge's decision, the competition and the condition of your dog compared to the others. By noting these things you can decide whether that judge is worth another entry from you. You'll be surprised at how quickly your file will build up.

But for now, you are ready to enter the ring.

IN THE RING

You have your armband affixed to your arm. Your dog has been brushed and exercised, so there is no chance that it will mess in the ring. You have its show lead on and you are ready to enter the ring. The judge will have told the steward whether the class is to be placed in numerical order, or in any way they wish to enter. Listen for the instructions and follow the other exhibitors. If there is competition and you are called in by numbers, you have no choice but to go where you are directed. If the judge does not care about the order, do not feel compelled to go in first. In fact, as a novice you will want to go to the back of the line so you can watch the other exhibitors as you move up the line.

Once you have become more proficient at handling and more observant of the competition, you should select a place between two dogs where yours will look good by comparison. For instance, if your dog has an excellent head, try to stand next to one with a poor head, so yours will stand out. If your dog is too big, don't put yourself next to one that is small.

Observation is the most important thing you can learn during your first ventures into the ring. Watch the judge as he or she walks down the line making first impressions. Be alert for the signal to gather your lead and prepare to circle the ring all together. Watch as the judge individually examines each dog. Does the judge gait each

The judge examines the head of an Irish Setter.

An exhibitor plays with Soft Coated Wheaten Terrier in the ring.

An exhibitor prepares to stack a Cocker Spaniel.

This handler has stacked a Wire Fox Terrier.

dog after it has been examined, or is the judge going over all the dogs and then gaiting them one by one?

If you are in the back of the line, you should notice the gaiting pattern. The judge will instruct the first person how the dog should be moved. It will be either straight down and back, in a triangle or in an L. The pattern will be the same for every person in the ring. If you are watching, you need only wait for the signal to move before going ahead. Some judges get pretty tired of exhibitors who have been paying no attention and must ask for instructions, when the same thing has been happening ten times before them.

Judges have different ways of sorting out a large class. Some judges make notes, some place the class as they go along, by instructing the exhibitor to go to the head of the line, to the foot of the line, or behind or in front of other exhibitors in the line. You must pay attention to where the judge wants you to go.

Often the judge will go over the exhibits, gait them and send them to the back of the line until every one has been examined. Then, in large classes, a selection process takes place. The judge will pull out the dogs he or she wants to keep, or sometimes the ones intended for dismissal. The judge will look them all over again, sometimes asking them to gait individually straight down and back. The ones no longer being considered after a second look are usually excused from the ring. The others remain for the judge to examine one more time.

Some judges place the entire class; others pull out only the first through fourth placements, sending them to the front of the line. The judge will then usually send the class around in a circle once more and then make his or her selections by pointing to the placements.

At this point, if you are still in the final group, keep one eye on the judge as you go around the ring. Sometimes a judge will point as you are running and you may miss the signal. It is embarrassing to have your fellow exhibitors push you up, or for the judge to have to walk down the line again to signal you out.

Granted, some judges are very imprecise in their instructions and their hand movements. Sometimes it appears as though they were waving to their friends at ringside instead of directing the class. Others are like drill sergeants, barking instructions and directing traffic. The happy medium is judges who are precise in expressing themselves, definite in their motions, yet courteous and considerate of the dogs and the exhibitors.

Sometimes exhibitors would like to know why a judge did not

An English Springer Spaniel is shown indoors on slippery mats.

This English Springer Spaniel is gaiting on grass.

place their dog. It is acceptable to ask a judge for a personal opinion after the breed has been completely judged. Judges vary about whether to express opinions outside of the class. Some are quite open and willing to discuss the relative merits of a dog. Others do not give opinions, and that is their prerogative. You have already been given the judge's opinion by whether or not your dog was placed in the class.

It is helpful to novices to learn from knowledgeable people about the quality of their animals, but more can be learned from talking to long-time, reputable breeders and those actively involved with the breed. If you have a good dog, people will tell you. If you do not, people will usually not tell you, but by their lack of enthusiasm it will become apparent. There are differences of opinion among fellow competitors as well. Breeding, showing and judging are all very subjective occupations, given to varying interpretations and outcomes. The uncertainty of it all is one of the reasons that it holds attractions and challenges for so many people.

Winners Class

After the judge has gone over every class of one sex, the winners of those classes return to compete for Winners Dog or Winners Bitch. If you have been lucky on that day and have won your class, you will go back into the ring when the steward calls for the class. Usually the steward will call out the numbers of the class winners. Dogs will set up in the ring with the Open Dog leading, followed by American Bred, Bred by Exhibitor, Novice, Twelve to Eighteen Months (only at Specialties) and Puppy.

The judge may go over each dog again individually and gait each one. The judge may then ask the class to circle once or twice before selecting the Winners Dog or Bitch. After the ribbon has been awarded, the Winner leaves the ring and the second-place winner in the class from which Winners Dog or Bitch was selected enters the ring to be judged along with the rest for Reserve Winners. As an example, if the Winners Dog comes from the Open class, then the second-place dog from Open comes in and stands at the head of the line for the judge to examine. If the Winners Dog comes from the Puppy class, the second-place puppy is then required to be presented for Reserve Winners competition. Although this does not happen very often, exhibitors should always be aware that it might occur and be prepared to rush back into the ring. One never knows from which class the judge will find the Winners Dog or Bitch.

Best of Breed

After all the classes have been judged and Winners Dog and Winners Bitch have been selected, the Specials class enters the ring. This class includes all the champions for that breed, plus the Winners Dog and Winners Bitch. These two may compete for Best of Breed and also with each other for Best of Winners.

In a large Specials class the judge may elect to divide the class, judging dogs and bitches separately. Usually Winners Dog and Winners Bitch are placed at the end of the line of Specials. However, the judge may elect to place the Winners Dog at the end of the dogs and do the same for the bitches. If your dog was chosen Winners Dog or Bitch, you must watch for the judge's instructions. When you enter the ring, if neither the judge nor the steward has directed you, it is proper to ask the steward where the judge wants to place the Winners Dog and Bitch. By doing this you call attention to your dog and make the judge aware of your presence.

The Specials class is judged exactly the same as the regular classes, with the judge circling the class, examining and gaiting each dog individually and finally selecting the Best of Breed, Best of Opposite Sex to Best of Breed and Best of Winners.

If the Winners Dog or Winners Bitch is chosen Best of Breed, that dog may gain additional points from defeating all the champions. The number of champions defeated is added to the number of dogs defeated in the regular classes. Although the formula appears to be complicated, it really is not. At the front of every show catalog the number of points being awarded that day for each breed is listed, so you can figure out how many points you will gain should you win on that day.

It is important when you are working toward a championship to keep track of the number of dogs actually shown, because absentees are not counted in the total number. You will hear conversation about one show or another having "majors." That means there are enough dogs so the winner will garner three or more points. One of the real faux pas in showing is to deliberately "break the major." Unless a real catastrophe strikes, it is very bad form not to show up when the entry schedule shows that there will be just enough for a major on that day.

This handler baits a Rhodesian Ridgeback.

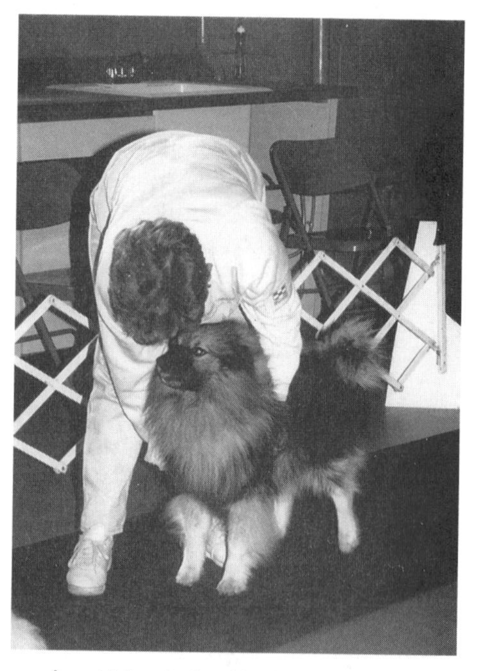

An exhibitor stacks a Keeshond on the mat.

The Group

If your dog has won Best of Breed, it will be eligible to enter Group competition. Groups are judged one at a time at most shows, although sometimes they are judged two at a time in the interest of allowing exhibitors to get home before midnight. At all major shows where there is a spectator gate, the Groups are judged singly. At a few shows, such as Westminster Kennel Club, they are judged in the evening and it becomes a formal occasion.

The order of Group judging is determined by the Superintendent, and depends largely on the judging schedule for the breeds. Groups cannot begin until all breeds in a particular group have been judged. If entries are large in one Group, that one will be scheduled later in the day.

Group judging is quite different from judging in the classes, because the judge has so many different breeds of dogs before him. In the Group, showmanship is very important. The dog must be in excellent condition and its attitude must be that of a true showman. Some people decry Group judging because dogs that may be better representatives of their breeds do not win because they lack the spark that sets them apart.

However, it is a dog *show,* and during Group and Best in Show competition, the *show* part is emphasized.

The only way to really prepare for Group competition is to watch the Groups in order to know the procedures and where your breed fits into the lineup. In addition, you must mentally prepare yourself and your dog to perform in a ring three times the size of a breed ring. The moves are the same, but novices will feel dwarfed and sometimes intimidated by the high-powered competition around them. You can reassure yourself by knowing that everyone in that ring began as you did, and you will also find that most competitors in the Group ring will be helpful and guide you along with the mechanics. They will not step aside for you in the lineup, circling or stacking your dog, however. You must be able to hold your own against competition.

Here is where your practice beforehand becomes essential. You must know all the moves, so they become almost automatic. You will become rattled if you are fishing for your lead, groping for your bait, tripping over your feet in your anxiety to do everything perfectly. Slow down all your motions, so you do not look like a Charlie Chaplin movie in fast forward. The tendency for the novice is to do everything in a fast and jerky fashion. Pretend that you are moving in slow motion and you will end up doing it just right. Practice until you can do everything smoothly and efficiently with a minimum of effort and wasted movement. The more you practice the more confident you will feel, and that confidence will be transmitted to your dog.

Best In Show

It does happen from time to time that the novice dog and novice handler wins the Group. When that occurs they must be prepared for the final competition of the day, Best in Show.

Seven dogs, representing each of the seven groups recognized by the AKC, compete for Best in Show. Judging takes place at the end of the day at most shows, when very few people are left to applaud the winner. At the biggest and most prestigious shows, this is not the case, and there is usually an enthusiastic crowd applauding their favorites in the ring.

This is where poise, confidence and showmanship play a major part. The dog must be turned on by the crowd, just as an actor is by an appreciative audience. You, as the pilot, are really along for the ride, guiding the dog through its paces, allowing the dog to show itself to its best advantage. This is the time when you have to know your dog's capabilities and enhance them. You cannot, however, lose control and allow the dog to make errors in gaiting or stacking.

In the Best in Show ring, the steward will indicate where the judge wants the exhibits to stand. Larger breeds are usually placed in front, just as in the Group ring; smaller breeds bring up the rear. The judge may want to see them circle together, and then they will be examined individually. The procedure is always the same. It is the tension and excitement that increases as you go from Breed to Group to Best in Show.

While you are waiting for Group and Best in Show judging, you must rest yourself and your dog. Have something to eat, allow the dog to drink and relieve itself before you put it on the table to brush it once again. Do not bring it to the ring too early, nor should you wait until the last second to rush breathlessly into the fray. Do everything in a timely and leisurely fashion until just before you go in. Then begin to encourage your dog, play a little with it, pique its enthusiasm with bait or a toy so it knows that what is about to happen is fun.

Every dog is different. As you and your dog become a team, you will be able to determine how much to spark its enthusiasm before going into the ring. Some dogs need lots of encouragement. Other dogs sense the excitement and get themselves so wrought up you will have to calm them down.

Seasoned show dogs know when their moment to shine occurs, and it is seeing that showmanship coupled with a competent handler that makes dog shows worth it all.

A competitor congratulates the winner in the Group ring.

12 Sportsmanship

SHOWING DOGS is unique among all sports because it is the only activity in which amateurs compete directly with professionals. When you are in the show ring, you are in competition with others like yourself, novices who show for the fun of it, and with handlers who make a living from showing dogs for others.

Under these circumstances, it is easy to blame someone else when your dog does not win. The "sour grapes" syndrome is alive and well in dogdom. But consider the facts. Professional handlers practice their craft. They know how to make a dog look good. They know how to accentuate its good points and hide its faults, but a knowledgeable judge knows those tricks, too. A good judge will find the worthy dogs, sometimes despite inept handling.

Professionals like to take dogs they can win with, because it enhances their reputation, so they will try to take dogs to show that are good specimens to begin with. Then they will condition and groom them properly and show them to their best advantage.

There are no hidden secrets in what a professional handler does. An owner can do the same thing, with the added advantage that the owner has to work with only one dog, whereas the professional has a whole string of dogs to consider. An owner who really wishes to compete must meet certain conditions. The dog must truly be worthy of winning; an owner with a mediocre dog will never beat a professional with a good dog, nor should they. In addition, the owner must be willing to put the time and the effort into training and conditioning that dog, both physically and mentally. Although some judges will find the good dog with the bad handler, many will not put out the effort to make your dog look good despite your ineptitude.

With one dog to concentrate on and the dedication to succeed, owner/handlers can win over the professional.

Professionals who care for their dogs and the sport that has given them a livelihood are generally willing to help a novice. They will give advice if they are asked. They will congratulate a novice if they win, and they will usually take defeat in good grace. A good professional will not knock the competition, at least in public.

Owner/handlers should do the same. Even if it hurts, go up to the competition that has just beaten you, shake hands and congratulate the winner. If you have placed in the class, but not as highly as you would have liked, take the ribbon, thank the judge and leave. If you were eliminated on the first cut, leave the ring with dignity. Don't storm out and do not badger the judge, or you may find yourself brought up on charges of poor sportsmanship before a disciplinary committee of the club. If you are the winner, don't gloat, don't tell the immediate world that yours is the best dog that ever walked. Just thank the judge politely for the win, accept good wishes from your competitors with modesty and retire to rest your dog and your feet.

Always keep your opinions to yourself when you are at ringside. Many people have been caught with foot-in-mouth when their disparaging comments have been overheard by a competitor's spouse whom they did not know was sitting beside them. Voices carry; bad news carries even faster. If you plan to get ahead in the dog game, keep your remarks positive or silent. This is especially true for the novice, whose opinion is not of great value to anyone, despite the high regard they may hold for themselves.

Professionals are generally very competitive people. That gives them an edge in winning. They do not like to lose any more than you do, but when they do, the true dog people will leave the ring, go back to their vans, roll up the windows and *then* express their disdain for the judging. There are great stories of professional handlers retreating to the showers after a particularly sobering defeat, consoling each other in the privacy of the stalls.

You will lose more often than you will win. That's the nature of dog shows. They are, after all, based on the opinion of a given judge on the day of the show. If you are of a temperament that cannot accept losses, perhaps you are in the wrong sport. Losing is part of the game, but if you have faith in your dog, a loss is not the end of the world. It is only the end of the day.

If you are losing despite everything that you are doing to hone your skills, it is perfectly acceptable to ask advice of anyone in your breed whom you have seen over a period of time, especially if they are winning. If there is a professional who regularly shows your breed, you can ask advice and it will usually be given graciously. Timing is important here. Do not approach anyone before they are going into a ring. At most, suggest that you would like to talk to them about your dog, and let them set the time. You may have to wait until the end of the day when classes are over, or you may catch them during an extended wait.

If you are given specific advice, follow it. That may seem to be a strange statement, but often novices believe that they know their dogs better than anyone and therefore the advice does not apply to them. This does not include the rare instance when a suggestion may include something shady, such as dyeing or altering a dog to make it conform better to the Standard.

The operative word in dog showing is "sport." It is the "sport of dogs," a phrase that sometimes seems to get lost in the heat of competition or the desire to own a top-winning specimen. Sometimes one becomes so discouraged that it almost seems futile to go on. When that happens, it is useful to take a little hiatus. Stay home for a while. Rest your dog. Work at getting it into better condition. Concentrate on your attitude and on your physical movements as you show your dog. Hone your skills.

Choose a show that you know is fun, where the venue is pleasant and the club goes all out to make the exhibitors feel comfortable, and where many of your breed are entered, so you will not be alone. Go to have a good time. Cultivate the attitude that winning is not everything, it is not even the only thing (to paraphrase a quote from famous football coach Vince Lombardi). Then if you lose, it is not the end of the world, and if you win, it's a bonus.

There is one other very important ingredient of showmanship for the owner/handler. The dog you bring into the ring is the same dog you will take home, whether you win or lose. If you believe the dog is good enough to compete, then you must have faith in it, even when you lose. Your belief in that dog, the dignity with which you handle it in the ring and afterwards must be the same. The dog does not care whether it wins or loses as long as it pleases you. Dogs know what is important. Sometimes owners need to learn their lessons from the other end of the lead.

"Sportsmanship!" That's the operative word.

13

The Career of the Show Dog

THE MAJORITY of show dogs finish their championships, or they do not, within two years. They go back to the couch to resume their lives as companions and pets to their loving owners. If it is a bitch, it may be bred once or twice. If it is a dog, the majority are never used by anyone except their owners. Their career ends with the final point, or when their owner becomes discouraged and quits.

There are those dogs and their owners, however, who do not quit, especially if that dog turns out to be a good one. An exceptional dog in any breed is an asset to that breed, and the owner may want to continue to show it as a Special. Both dogs and bitches can compete successfully as Specials. In a coated breed, it is more difficult to campaign a bitch than a dog, since bitches may not carry as much coat and tend to blow their coats after they have been in season. Bitches, however, have had spectacular show careers, winning Groups and Bests in Show at some of the world's most prestigious events.

If you decide to Special your dog, you must have a clear goal in mind, because the race to the top of the rating systems can depend on no more than one or two wins. Specialing is very expensive, whether you do it yourself or hire a professional. Doing it yourself is cheaper, once you get into the Group and Best in Show wins, but your success may be limited by the competition you will encounter. Specialing a dog as an owner/handler requires an added measure of dedication and work for both you and your dog.

Not only will you incur expenses traveling around the country, but you will find that it is lonely at the top. You'll have your supporters who believe in you and in your dog, but you will also find a great many detractors, some in other breeds, some in your own breed. You will need absolute faith in your dog and in your own ability to present it properly.

Owner/handlers have a better chance of becoming number one in their breed than they do in winning the most numbers of Groups in the country, or the most Bests in Show. Logistically, it requires such an effort to travel to all the big shows and to be out fifty-two weeks a year for two, sometimes three or four shows a week that it really does require professional dedication to devote that much time to showing a dog. In addition to the time and expense, the dog must have extraordinary mental and physical stamina to go that distance for one year, not to mention the two or three years that it takes to break records.

As an owner/handler you must set your sights on an achievable goal and then plan your year with that goal in mind. You may decide to win the most Best of Breeds, or to defeat the greatest number of dogs in your breed. The two are not necessarily the same, though they often are. As an example, in an area where there are quite a few shows but with small entries, you may win the most Breeds, but not defeat more dogs than someone who lives in a region where entries are consistently large. Your own circumstances will dictate what a reasonable goal for your dog should be. You may set your sights on winning the National Specialty, or the three or four most prestigious shows in the United States. Whatever it is, be prepared for a year of hard work, some great wins and bitter losses.

Specialing requires a rock-solid relationship with your dog. You must be attuned to every nuance of its behavior and health. You must know how to make it look its best under all conditions. If you have never used a video camera, now is the time. Ask a friend, a spouse or a child to video you as you stack and gait your dog, both at home and at shows, indoors and outdoors. You will be amazed at what you see through the camera's eye. It will help you correct your own mistakes and consequently those you are fostering in your dog. The

A little pre-show conversation between Irish Setter and owner.

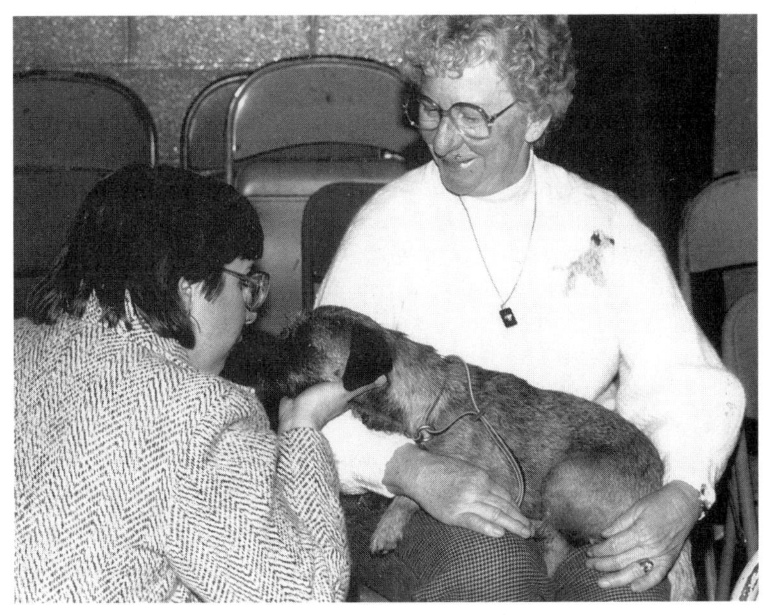

This Border Terrier enjoys a lap.

camera will show you what the judge sees in a way that you have never been able to detect before.

As you go through a year of showing your dog, you will have to be creative about what is needed to keep it happy and interested in the ring. Some show dogs are natural actors. They turn on for the crowd. Those are the easy ones. Those who tend to get bored doing the same thing every week will need other incentives. They are often the smart dogs, who must be given a reason to be on their toes on command.

Some handlers solve this problem by using special treats only in the ring. Others give the dog attention and affection only in the ring—a difficult program to follow if your champion is also your companion at home. There are many tricks of the trade. By observation and experimenting with your dog, you will devise some of your own.

Once you have set your sights on a goal and have determined that your dog is of the right age and in optimum condition, you can plan your strategy. There are calendars put out by some of the dog food companies that list every all-breed show in the country for the year. In addition, the AKC publishes a list of all the shows, both all-breed and Specialties, for the year. By saving your events calendar supplement to the *AKC Gazette* for one year you can determine every show and its corresponding date for the year, and by saving your awards section of the *AKC Gazette* you can determine which shows are likely to have big entries in your breed, based on the year before.

There's no doubt that planning a show career involves saving lots of paper that you might ordinarily throw away. Don't! Keep all your records and those of your competition from the time you begin your show career until that dog is retired. Check your winning records and the number of dogs defeated against those published in the *AKC Gazette* awards section. Occasionally one of you will make a mistake, and you will need to verify your win, since one dog may make a difference in whether or not you achieve your goal.

SPECIALING BITCHES

If you are campaigning a bitch, you will probably want to delay breeding her until the year is over. This is a decision you will have to make ahead of time. It will depend on her age at the time you plan to Special her, on how well she holds her coat and condition after her heat, how often during the year she comes into heat. If she is approaching four, you may have to plan on showing her until her next heat, as you don't want to breed a maiden bitch too much later than four. After that age she may encounter uterine problems, and the size of litters tends to decrease. When she comes into heat, if you know she will drop every hair, you might as well breed her, since you can't show her, anyway. If she comes in only once every year or ten months, you will have to decide, based on her age and condition, whether to forgo showing or breeding.

While you are out campaigning, you have a good opportunity to evaluate possible mates for your bitch. Never choose a sire based on his winning record. Choice of a mate should always be done on the basis of what is correct for your bitch. Never breed to a dog with a major fault. Never duplicate faults by breeding to a dog with the same fault as your bitch. Select a sire on the basis of phenotype and genotype—looks and pedigree. He should be a good representative of the breed, with no major inheritable faults and with a pedigree that, when blended with that of your bitch, will hopefully bring out the best qualities of both. Genetics being the imprecise science that it is, in dog breeding, at least, "hope" is as good a qualifier as anything. Being able to see some of his produce, especially if they come from similar bloodlines, is also helpful.

If your bitch finishes when she is quite young, say under three years old, she may not be ready to be Specialed. In that case you may decide to breed her first and show her later. Breeding will mature her body and will, in most cases, not hinder her at all from being shown after she is back in condition.

Sometimes, in slow-maturing breeds, it is advisable to breed a bitch at her third season, usually about two and a half years old, before she is ever shown. If a bitch needs greater depth of chest or rib spring, having a litter of puppies will usually help that maturity, and you can start her show career after the puppies are born and she is back in shape.

SPECIALING DOGS

Showing a dog is quite different from showing a bitch as a Special. Generally males carry more coat, may be more impressive to look at and may possess a greater degree of showmanship than some bitches. That is not to say that everything else can be forgotten.

Not at all! The dog, if anything, must be in glowing condition, mentally and physically alert, and on top of his form at every show. While bitches may be a little moody, dogs can be easily distracted by bitches in heat or other males around them, and in most cases, you will have to work harder to motivate a male than a bitch. In the large breeds, your own physical stamina needs to be greater as you set about achieving your goal.

Males do not need time out to breed, but their coats will go through seasonal fluctuations. If yours is a coated breed, you will need to keep it in a temperature- and light-controlled environment. This is also true for bitches, but since they will shed no matter what because of their hormones, this advice is directed primarily at the boys.

The amount of hair growth of any dog is dependent upon temperature and light. Dogs in warm climates never grow the undercoat that dogs in northern climes do, unless they are kept in air conditioning all the time. Hair growth is also dependent upon the amount of daylight. The longer the nights, the more the hair grows. During the summer, when the days are longest, hair grows the least amount. Some professional handlers keep the amount of light constant throughout the year by artificial means. They either put the dogs to bed earlier in the summer, maintaining the dark, or keep the lights on in the kennel to the same time each day. In addition, it is important to keep new coat coming in by stripping out the old coat daily.

Nutrition is vital to good coat production, and you may have to experiment with various types of feed in order to find the one which promotes the best and most luxurious growth. There are also many supplements that claim to grow coat. Some of these may be helpful, but you will have to try them out. Some people claim great success with nothing more than the addition of safflower oil or egg yolks to the diet. Everyone has a pet remedy, and most people are willing to share their secret successes with you.

BREEDING AND SHOWING

As you campaign your dog and it is seen at the shows, you may get requests for stud service. This can be flattering for the novice owner, but also requires an enormous amount of responsibility both to your dog and to the bitch.

The axiom is: If the puppies turn out beautiful, it is due to the bitch; if they turn out horrible, the dog is certainly to blame. No bitch owner is ever going to admit that her prized animal produces terrible puppies! Therefore, it behooves you, as the stud dog owner, to allow only good bitches with compatible pedigrees to breed to your dog. The temptation of earning the stud fee is compelling, but should not be so enticing as to destroy your dog's reputation as an excellent sire. The same rules apply for dogs and bitches, and also the same precautions.

Always insist upon a veterinary certificate stating that the dog or bitch has been tested for brucellosis, mycoplasma and other sexually transmitted diseases and has been found negative for all of them. Infection by one of these diseases can render a dog or a bitch permanently sterile. It is a stiff price to pay for allowing even one animal to waive the rules. Do not allow the dog or bitch to wait until the last moment before her season to have tests done. Some of them take several days to be analyzed, and the results can come too late. As the owner of the stud dog you will want to protect his health, and as the owner of the bitch you will want to assure a healthy litter and a dam able to take care of them properly.

Using a dog at stud while it is being campaigned involves great logistics. Sometimes the deed is consummated at a show where both are conveniently present. More likely, however, the bitch will be flown to the nearest airport in the dead of night on Christmas Eve, and you, as the responsible recipient of someone's precious animal, are duty bound to get to the airport and rescue her. You will also be responsible for keeping her safe while in your custody, consummating one or two breedings, and shipping her out when the time comes.

Every arrangement between stud dog and brood bitch should be in writing. Determine in advance what the stud fee will be, when it is due to be paid and what happens if the bitch misses. There are no fast rules about stud fees. Some dog owners ask for the money at the time of service. Others ask for half at the service and half when the puppies are whelped. Still others ask for a stud fee only when there are a certain number of live puppies in the litter. If the bitch misses, it is customary to give a return service. If that is not desired by either party, then any money paid is kept by the stud owner. If the stud owner wants pick of the litter instead of a fee, that should be spelled out in writing as well. Specify dog or bitch puppy, and at what age you would like to receive your puppy.

If the dog refuses to breed the bitch, the stud owner receives no

A Malamute puppy and a Norwich Terrier converse with their owner.

Nose to Nose.

money, no matter whose fault it is. It is customary, however, for the owner of the bitch to pay shipping charges both ways and any board incurred while she is waiting to be bred.

All of these arrangements should be made well in advance and be agreeable to both parties.

RETIREMENT

Now you have your Special, your stud dog or brood bitch, and the temptation is strong to forget how it all began. The career of a show dog is short, three years at the most, but that dog will be a part of your life for many years to come. As a brood bitch her maternal duties will not extend much beyond six or seven years old. Stud dogs can sire puppies many years past that age as long as they remain in good health. But through all those years, the dog that launched you into the show ring will still be your companion and will want to accompany you as you set out with a new puppy.

You may find that when your champion is left at home it will actually become depressed. Shows will have become a way of life for it, and to be replaced by an upstart is difficult for anyone, dog or human. You can ease this burden by taking it along occasionally, or by entering a new phase of achievement. You can begin training for the Obedience ring. Many Conformation champions do very well in Obedience, especially since it means they will be going out once again with you. Many retired champions go to National Specialties as Veterans, so that new exhibitors have an opportunity to see the great dogs that have gone before.

Even such mundane excursions as trips to the shopping center to be walked around and admired give a psychological lift to the retired champion.

It is important for both of you to keep up the grooming and general health care that many people neglect once the dog is finished with its show career. Keep your old champion looking good while you move on to the new hopeful.

Your first champion was your learning dog. You made all your mistakes on it. It deserves your loyalty and a special place in your heart.

REDEFINING YOUR GOALS

After you have finished your first dog, bred your first litter or put a dog out to stud, you are no longer a novice. That does not mean that you know everything, or that there is no more to learn. The world of the purebred dog is endlessly fascinating to those caught up in it. At some point during those first couple of years you will have to take stock and perhaps redefine the goals you set for yourself when you began. There are many who are satisfied with their one champion, and they disappear from view to enjoy their dog and to get on to other things in their lives. Studies have shown that the average life of a dog show fancier is five years, approximately the time it takes to buy a puppy, raise it, show it, possibly breed it and then move along to other interests. For those who are truly bitten by the "show bug," however, the questions of what comes next invariably arise. For those who love the sport, there is a void when one has nothing left to show, and from that emptiness comes the next generation of breeders and exhibitors.

The question is whether to breed a litter and keep a puppy to show, or whether to buy a new puppy with the intent to show it, and possibly breed that new generation. Either way, you are on the track of becoming a multiple-dog household.

If your first champion was a bitch, then you most probably will breed her and keep a puppy from that litter. That will be the beginning of your line. If your first was a dog, then you have the choice of taking a stud puppy, leasing a bitch from a good breeder or buying a bitch outright, either to breed to your dog or to raise, show and breed to something compatible with her. Any move you make requires some long-range planning.

If you decide to breed your bitch, the choice of the sire, the selection of a puppy from the litter, the seemingly endless wait for the puppy to grow up and show its potential, all require dedication and patience. Breeding good-quality dogs is the foundation of the purebred dog fancy. Some people seem to have an affinity for that aspect of the sport. They would rather be breeders than either exhibitors or judges. Their greatest joy is to combine the genes of two animals and come up with a dog of superior qualities that someone can then take and mold into a show dog.

There are others who do not have either the time or the temperament to be good breeders. Those people would do better to buy their next dog and bring it along, taking advantage of their experience with the first.

Whatever your interest, the knowledge you have gained by showing your own dog, the friends you have made and the experiences you have enjoyed will stand you in good stead as you take the next step.

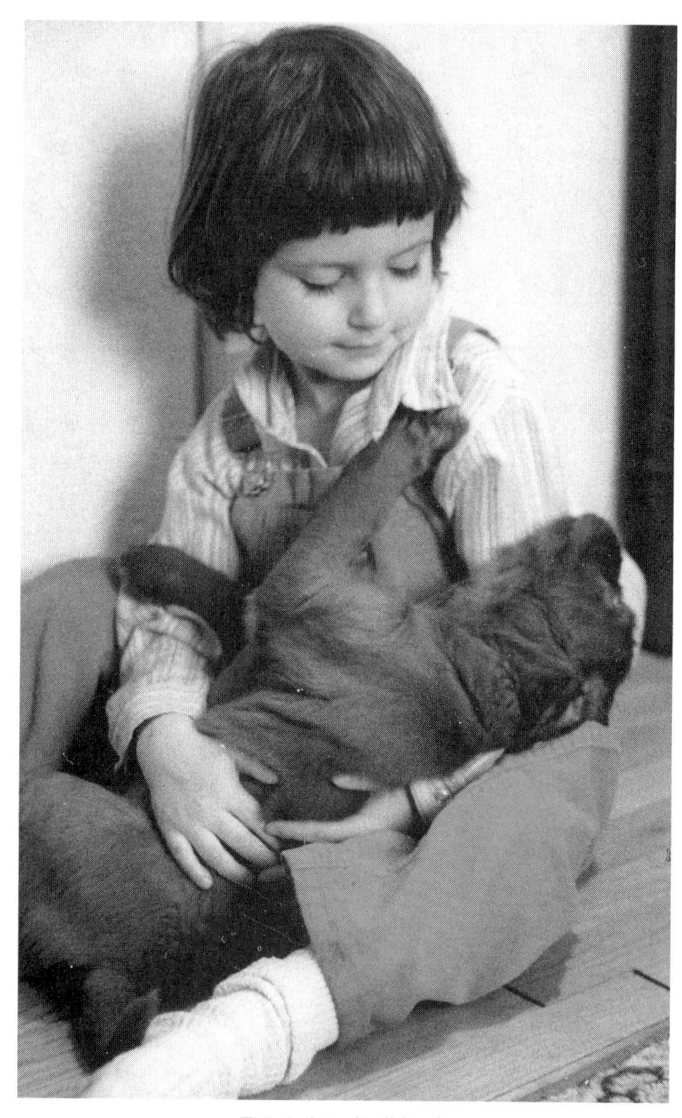

This is how it all begins.

14

Junior Showmanship: The Next Generation

DOG SHOWING is a family sport, whether you go initially just to look at the different breeds before you select one, or whether you take the children along because there is no one at home to watch them. Kids are everywhere at dog shows, and if you go often enough with your children, they will develop their own coterie of friends to keep them amused. Exposure to dog shows is how most children become involved in Junior Showmanship.

At its best, classes for children teach them many things about responsibility for their dogs, good sportsmanship and knowledge about the care of an animal. At their worst, they reflect in miniature every bad aspect of dog showing from grumpy judges to poor sportsmanship to disregard for the animals themselves. With proper parental guidance, however, children can become happily and productively involved in the sport.

Children can be taught all the basics of good handling with the dog you are showing. It is easier for a child to take a small dog into the ring, rather than one that towers over it, but even that can be done, so long as the dog is well mannered. Many children prevail upon their parents to get them a dog of their own, and in many ways

Setting up a Beagle.

How's that, Dad?

that is a good idea. If the child is given responsibility for daily care, grooming and training of its own dog for the show ring, he or she will take the whole experience seriously, whereas if all the child needs to do is to walk into the ring with mom or dad's dog, it will mean little.

Classes are held at most shows for juniors divided by age and experience. Children must be ten years of age and may compete in Junior Showmanship until they are eighteen. Classes are held for novice and experienced juniors, also separated by age. Juniors are judged by their handling skills only. The dogs are not evaluated, and all breeds are shown together. Judges are expected to determine how well the child manages the dog, whether the child is in control, shows poise and is able to present the dog to its best advantage.

Ring procedure is the same as for any other class. The judge will bring the class in, circle the dogs, examine and gait each one individually and then place them. In cases where the judge is undecided, the two or three in competition will be asked to gait or to free-bait, or to demonstrate in some fashion that they are actively showing their dogs.

Children are expected to act in a sportsmanlike manner. Winners should graciously accept their awards. Losers should congratulate the winners, just as their elders should do in the regular classes.

Parents often become overbearing with their children. This is certain to discourage a child, and may turn a budding assistant or junior handler away from the sport permanently. If a child makes a mistake in the ring, it will learn to do better next time only if corrected in private after the class is over. Learning by example is very important in handling. The child needs to be shown precisely how to perform a certain maneuver in the ring, and should practice in advance. It is more difficult for a child and a dog to work as a team than for an adult and a dog, because the child's concentration is usually lacking. It is best to keep lessons short and always end them on a positive note. Young children's movements tend to be jerky and uncoordinated; they should be taught to slow their actions down so what they do looks smooth and graceful. A minimum of motion of hands, arms and feet makes a better impression on the judge and will calm a nervous dog. Showing a dog takes good hand/eye coordination, and daily practice will help a youngster develop those skills.

Lessons should be short, but if possible done every day. Practice should be required, just as it is mandatory in any other sport in which a child becomes involved.

Children tend to become impatient and hard-handed with a dog if it does not behave perfectly. This should *never* be allowed. *Children must be forbidden to strike a dog under any conditions.*

Parents often become discouraged and disappointed when their children lose interest in dog shows in favor of other sports, or other activities. Dog shows should not be projected onto the child as an extension of the parent. Those who have a true aptitude and enjoy it will choose it over other options. Children who drift away should not be forced to participate. Often they will take up more exciting pastimes, but what they have learned has benefited them, nonetheless. Many children return to the show ring eventually, sometimes not until they are older and show in the regular classes, but those who learn at an early age will remember their experiences and skills.

Many professional handlers started in the Junior Showmanship ring. Junior competition was first begun in the late 1920s under the impetus of Leonard Brumby, Sr., a noted kennel manager, professional handler and later AKC executive. It was mostly an East Coast phenomenon, with the first recorded children's handling class held at the Westbury Kennel Club show in 1932. Eventually children's handling caught on at other shows throughout the country, and its name was changed to Junior Handling and eventually Junior Showmanship.

SPECIAL LIMITED COMPETITION FOR JUNIORS

Today's junior competition is keen with one impetus provided by the Westminster Kennel Club show and other large shows. In order to compete at Westminster, a junior must have won eight first-place ribbons at shows during the previous year. The incentive to qualify for the limited shows has encouraged juniors to do their best throughout the year. It is not easy to win over all competition in one's class at eight different shows, so in order to achieve this goal, juniors are showing more than they might ordinarily.

Another competition for juniors involves winning first place at major designated shows in order to compete at a national championship event held annually in conjunction with an important all-breed show. The winner of that competition is given a trip to compete in the World Junior Showmanship competition, which is held in conjunction with the Crufts Dog Show in England. This entire enterprise is underwritten by one of the pet food companies.

Golden Retriever and her young handler.

The Best Junior in Show shares her award with a friend.

Show-giving clubs customarily either waive the fee for juniors if the dog is also entered in another class, or they charge reduced fees for juniors in order to encourage more of them to be able to compete.

Occasionally conflicts arise if the dog is entered in either obedience or conformation, in addition to Junior Showmanship. It is a good idea to discuss the course of action with your junior before this impasse arises.

In the case of obedience, unless the dog is called for long sits or downs with the rest of the class, judges have the option of delaying its turn in the ring if a junior is in the ring. Obedience competition cannot be delayed past the last dog in the class, however.

If there is a conflict between conformation and juniors, the decision must be made in advance which one to choose. The factors to be weighed might be whether by pulling a dog out of its regular class it will be breaking a major, or whether this is the eighth show needed for the child to qualify for Westminster. Whatever the decision, it should be discussed ahead of time, so the child will not be surprised at the last minute and become discouraged. A child cannot be made to feel like a second-hand citizen at every show, and yet a junior must understand that there are times when it becomes more important to go into the conformation ring. Arguments at ringside, tears and recriminations do not make for happy dog show experiences for either child or parent, so potential problems should be aired before the classes are scheduled to be called. By reading your judging schedule in advance of going to the show you can usually determine whether a conflict will arise.

Juniors must show dogs owned by them or by a member of their immediate family and are listed in the catalog, so there is no possibility of grabbing a dog at ringside to borrow for the day.

Junior showmanship judges are approved and published in the same manner as conformation or obedience judges. There are rules governing the judging of those classes, and a special booklet developed by the AKC provides guidelines for the judging of juniors. Anyone competing in this class should know the guidelines, which are available from the AKC, in order to understand what judges will be looking for as they evaluate a class.

Many good times are had and long-standing friendships made through the associations of junior handlers getting together with a common interest. While some parents may secretly feel that getting a junior involved means finding reliable kennel help, it does not usually work that way. Your ambitions and those of your child should be kept separate, so that neither of you ends up feeling like a slave to the other with the dog as the pawn in the middle.

Parents and children alike should remember that dog showing is a sport, and the rules of good sportsmanship apply to both. Children and puppies are the future, to be nurtured and taught, fussed over and praised. The toddler in the stroller becomes a gawky teenager and eventually a mature adult. The bouncy puppy becomes a gangly adolescent who is transformed into a swan. For dog fanciers the two lives parallel in so many ways, linked by love and concern, joy and sorrow. Through all our lives there will be the human family and the canine family as generations of both succeed each other. For dog fanciers, the two become inseparable in a continuing stream of time—kids and dogs, dogs and kids, the best of all our days.

George Alston shows Irish Setter, Ch. McCamon Marquis to one of his many Best in Show wins.
Gilbert

15

The Professional Handler

THERE MAY COME A TIME when the owner of a show dog considers the possibility of using a professional handler. There are many perfectly good reasons for employing a professional.

Some people find after being in the ring week after week that they are simply physically unable to keep up the pace. Dog showing, even for the Toy breeds, requires a certain amount of athleticism, and one may find that the back and the knees cannot do the mind's bidding after a while. Many breeds, such as Afghan Hounds and German Shepherd Dogs, require the fitness of a long distance runner to show properly. While your goal may be to get in shape, the reality is that you won't.

Dog showing takes time, weekends of time, which means that things you did in your former life (before dog shows) are neglected. Eventually someone has to paint the house, rake the leaves, plant the garden, vacuum the rugs, change the oil and even go to a child's graduation or wedding! Don't laugh! Many a wedding has been planned around a National Specialty, and one breed club changed its annual weekend date to avoid graduations in June. So there are times when you just can't get to the shows and your dog is ready.

Expense is a consideration. It may appear to be less expensive to show your own dog, and if you go only once in a while and never travel more than a day trip away, then it is less expensive to show your own dog. However, if you go often, even two weekends a month, to a place requiring overnight accommodations, you will find that employing a handler to show your dog in the classes is usually cheaper. This must be qualified, because handlers charge different rates and have various other charges added on to the basic handling fee, which runs up the cost and which differ from one to another.

WHAT IS A PROFESSIONAL HANDLER?

Until the late 1940s there were no handlers who worked the way professionals do today. Until World War II the sport of dogs was dominated by a relatively small group of wealthy patrons who ran large kennels, specializing primarily in a single breed. These people hired kennel managers, often bringing them from Great Britain, where the tradition of stockmen who managed the landowner's horses and dogs went back hundreds of years.

These managers also served as handlers in the show ring for the kennels at which they were employed. They were knowledgeable dog men who often planned the breedings, bought and sold dogs for the kennel, ran the operation and by their skills brought prominence to many of the great lines of dogs that still exist today in many of the breeds. The offspring of these managers usually found employment or apprenticeship at other kennels.

After World War II the lavish style of the big kennels no longer prevailed, and the kennel managers who worked for one employer established their own kennels and began to show a variety of dogs for individual clients. During the 1950s and 1960s there was a proliferation of professional handlers, most of whom were schooled in the ways of their fathers.

In the early 1940s the American Kennel Club began licensing professional handlers in order to maintain standards of health for the dogs and business ethics for the clients. Until the early 1970s there were only a small number of professionals who were licensed by the AKC. They had to have served an apprenticeship, to have displayed a knowledge of business and demonstrated their professionalism in a limited number of breeds before they were approved. In the beginning handlers were licensed breed by breed, until the whole procedure became too cumbersome and unconditional licenses were granted.

In 1974 the AKC gave up licensing professional handlers because of the increasing numbers of people applying and the unwieldy nature of the rules. Many believe that the sport of dogs was dealt a grave blow by this deregulation. Once the restrictions were lifted, anyone with a leash and a comb could consider themselves a professional. Under the old AKC rules, only licensed handlers could charge a fee for handling a dog. Once the rules were discarded, anyone could charge, and a new category of handler, calling themselves "agents," was created. Agents are self-appointed handlers who guide a dog's career, or simply take it into the ring occasionally. The ranks of those calling themselves handlers or agents has swelled from several hundred to several thousand in the past fifteen years.

Two professional organizations have attempted to impose some regulations and restrictions on membership. The Professional Handlers Association was slow in filling the void created by the AKC, but it admits to membership only those who pass fairly strict criteria. They must have been handling for ten years, five as a professional, and have established kennel facilities. They must provide their clients with rate cards and contracts. The PHA attempts to attract those professional handlers who are interested in making dogs a full-time livelihood.

The Dog Handlers Guild is an organization of professional handlers primarily in the Midwest. Their membership is not as restrictive as the PHA, but they attempt to control their membership through a Code of Ethics. Both organizations have the means in their charter to discipline or expel those who violate their rules.

Today the professionalism has been blurred by people who show dogs for money but do not maintain established kennels and who have other jobs during the week. The ranks of the full-time professional who learned about dogs by apprenticing to others are thinning rapidly, but there are still some who have come up the old way and who devote their lives to dogs.

CHOOSING A PROFESSIONAL HANDLER

Prior to selecting someone to substitute for you in the ring, for that is what you do when you hire a professional handler, you must decide what you want of this person. Do you want someone who will take the dog at ringside and show it for you occasionally? Do you want a person to take the dog every week, but you will still keep it at home and bring it to the handler at ringside before judging? Are you interested in having the handler take the dog home, maintain it in the kennel, groom it and show it until it finishes its championship before returning the dog to you? Finally, do you want the handler to actively campaign the dog after it finishes its championship for a period of time?

You should have some idea of what you expect the handler to do before you approach anyone to show your dog. Giving the professional a clear picture of what you want will enable them to tell you what they will be able to do for your dog.

"Look before you leap" is the best advice in selecting a handler. Observe those handlers who are familiar with your breed both in the ring and outside. Notice how they interact with their dogs. Do they appear interested in them, concentrating on them, or are they busy chatting with their friends outside the ring? Do they treat the dogs with respect, or do they manhandle them, talk roughly or jerk them around? Take particular note of the condition of the dogs that a professional brings into the ring, especially those dogs who live at the kennel and for whose care the handler is responsible. Sometimes an owner brings a dog to ringside in poor condition or badly groomed, but there is never an excuse for that if responsibility for the dog's well-being has been delegated to the professional.

Walk around to the handler's van or motor home. Observe your dog's home-away-from-home. It should be well maintained, clean, free of trash, with ample room for adequate-sized crates and all the other equipment needed to carry the dogs comfortably. The vehicle should be in good repair, with tires that can withstand heavy travel over hazardous roads. The ventilation should be ample, with windows, vents and air-conditioning ducts that reach the recesses of the van, as well as the driver's seat.

Does the handler bring assistants along to help prepare dogs for the ring and to care for them while the show is in progress? Usually handlers carry at least one assistant, depending upon the number of dogs entered at a show. Sometimes the assistant will be called upon to handle a dog if the professional is occupied in another ring. The assistant is a very important part of a handler's retinue. That person is entrusted with the care, feeding and exercise of the dogs, and therefore has as much or more contact with them on a daily basis. The assistant is as close to an apprentice as one can find in the business today. Most professional handlers started out as assistants in someone's kennel before striking out on their own. Although the ultimate responsibility for your dog lies with the handler, you must feel comfortable with the assistants who will be caring for your dog.

Handlers and their dogs establish rapport after they have been together. During your observations try to determine whether the handler and the dogs work as a team. Not every dog is in the kennel long enough to bond to the handler, but those dogs who are there for months (sometimes years, if the dog is being campaigned as a Special) should work enthusiastically as part of a team.

Sportsmanship is another indication of a good handler. Is his or her ring etiquette good? You do not want to be associated with handlers who badger the judge, complain about losing, annoy the competition in the ring or in any way behave in an embarrassing manner.

Recommendations are another way of narrowing down the selection of a handler. Talk to people who have used those professionals you are considering. Find out if they are satisfied with the service and the consideration their dogs have received. Has the handler been honest about their dogs and in their business relationships?

Rapport between dog and handler is important. Equally important is rapport between client and handler. That confidence is built on trust, respect and honesty.

You are entrusting one of your most precious possessions, your dog, to this person. You should expect to be dealt with honestly, and your wishes respected. Conversely, the handler should be able to rely on your word and your sense of responsibility handling the finances incurred in showing your dog.

Once you have decided upon a handler, make an appointment to meet the handler after his or her duties for the day are over. Ask for an honest evaluation of your dog, and tell the handler what you wish to accomplish. If you intend to show the dog yourself and employ a handler occasionally, be up-front and state that. If you wish to send the dog with the handler, find out if that person is free to take the dog, or is committed to another dog in your breed. Handlers who are popular within breeds often line up their clients depending upon which dogs are ready to be shown at certain times. If you have a young dog, you might be willing to wait for an opening. If not, you may have to look elsewhere. Often handlers will take two of the same breed, but of opposite sexes. They may take an Open Dog and an Open Bitch, for instance, plus a Special. Occasionally they may take

A handler's motor home would be your dog's home-away-from-home.

Kennel runs should be clean and sturdy.

dogs in additional classes at all-breed shows, and usually they will take several class dogs at Specialties. They should not take two dogs in the same class, nor should they commit themselves to two Specials at the same time. Obviously, they cannot handle two dogs in the same class, so one of them would be given to the assistant or to another handler. If this is satisfactory to you, then you have no problem. If not, you must state clearly that you do not want anyone else taking your dog into the ring.

One of the stickiest problems between handlers and clients is that of conflicts in the ring. Handlers do not control the judging schedule, and inevitably there are occasions when the handler should be two places at once. You should discuss beforehand what happens when the handler encounters a conflict. How are the dogs covered? Usually, if the handler has a competent assistant, that will be the person to go into the ring with the dog with the hope that the handler will be finished with one assignment and take over. There is no guarantee that will happen in any class, however, so you must be prepared for that eventuality. Occasionally a handler will ask another professional to take the dog, and often that works out quite well. If you are committed to the idea that no one but the person you hired is to take your dog into the ring, you must state that clearly. In that event, your dog will not be shown that day, and you should not be charged the handling fee.

The Kennel

If you decide to send your dog out with a handler, you should make an effort to visit the kennel. This is where your dog will spend the majority of its time away from home, and you should determine if the facilities meet your expectations.

The kennel may be large and elaborate, or small and spare, but regardless of the size it should be spotlessly clean and well maintained. The place should smell sanitary, the runs should be picked up, no matter what time of day you arrive, and they should be of adequate size for a dog to exercise itself.

Kennel runs are usually surfaced with either concrete or stone. Stone runs must be replenished frequently and should look as though they were recently raked over and cleaned. Concrete runs must be hosed down daily and should be equipped with good drainage to allow runoff.

The inside stalls should be scrubbed and clean and of sufficient

A kennel/barn complex provides good space with indoor and outdoor facilities.

size for the dogs to rest comfortably. Fresh water should be available at all times.

Handlers have their own routines for exercising, feeding and grooming. You may wish to inquire about this. If your dog has special nutritional needs, discuss them with the handler. Usually they will wish to put your dog on the diet that has worked for their other clients, but in the case of allergies, or a food your dog dislikes, exceptions should be made.

Handlers should be willing to medicate dogs according to their owners' instructions for such things as heartworm preventative.

At the time of your visit discuss veterinary care in case of illness or emergencies. The handler should have an ongoing relationship with a veterinarian in the area and be willing to take responsibility for the dog's welfare. You will be charged for veterinary care and also for any special tests the handler may deem necessary for your dog. If your dog is a kennel resident for more than one month, the handler should have it tested for internal parasites. Some handlers routinely test monthly. You will be charged for this and for any medication, in the event that the dog needs to be treated.

Kennel help is extremely important. Just as the assistant is responsible for your dog's care on the road, the kennel help, which often includes the assistant as well, is charged with the day-to-day management of dogs in the kennel. They should be knowledgeable and, at the least, fond of animals.

Kennels are designed basically in two ways. One is equipped with indoor/outdoor runs, so the dogs have access during the day. Some have dog doors, so the dogs can go in and out at will. Most do not, however, and the dogs are let in and out during specified times by lifting or lowering the doors to the runs.

The second type of kennel arrangement is called a walk-out kennel. The runs are not connected to the indoor stalls and dogs must be physically walked out to their runs several times a day. The advantage to this type of run is that every dog is handled several times a day, so if a dog is sick or lame the problem will be spotted almost immediately.

Some kennels that do general boarding in addition to their show clients have two kennel buildings, one for the show dogs and one for boarders. The boarding kennel may be equipped with indoor/outdoor runs and the show kennel building may have walk-out runs. Usually handlers try to separate their general boarders from the show dogs to avoid the spread of illness that may be brought in by a pet. Conversely, dogs may bring back viruses from the shows that the kennel owner does not wish to spread into the boarding kennel.

The spread of disease is always a real threat in any situation where numbers of dogs are kept in close quarters. Since ventilation is a very important part of controlling viruses, the kennel should be well ventilated, with circulating fans and a flow of fresh air. Some kennels are air conditioned, as well as heated. In some climates this is a necessity, but unless the climate is very hot and muggy on a continuing basis, most handlers prefer not to use it. Going from air conditioning outside to the runs is more of a shock for the dog than to have it acclimatized to the prevailing conditions.

Since show dogs must perform in the heat, they do better in a natural environment unless it becomes a hardship.

Cleanliness, ventilation, maintenance and help are the elements of a good kennel. The ability to run one is one of the criteria of a good professional handler.

Fees

Professional handlers should provide their clients with clearly understandable rate cards. Rates for handling vary greatly from $25 for a young handler who walks your dog into the ring to $60 for a top professional. Specialty shows are more, from $75 to $100. In addition, most handlers charge a bonus for winning a Group or Best in Show. There are also charges for grooming, boarding and travel expenses. The latter are prorated among the number of dogs going on a particular trip. Some handlers charge an up-front amount for new clients.

All of these charges should be spelled out in advance, so there are no surprises when the bills start coming in. By knowing how much it will cost for a handler to show your dog, you can estimate what services you will need and whether you can afford them.

In the final analysis, after all the tangible factors are weighed, it comes down to personal rapport. Rapport between the dog and handler, and between handler and client. Once you have found that, the rest becomes easy.

Appendix

WE HAVE INCLUDED sample contracts you may use as guidelines. Also included is a sample entry form for any AKC Licensed show.

Each breeder, stud owner or professional handler emphasizes certain things. Therefore, it may be that no two contracts are alike. Purebred dogs are still very much a "handshake" business, but to protect both buyer and seller, client and handler, and above all, the dog, the AKC advises people to have written contracts so there will be no surprises down the road.

Additionally, you will find a chart explaining the format of a dog show.

PUPPY BUYER/SELLER CONTRACT

The breeder (named) hereby conveys ownership of puppy X out of a litter (Ch. Fido ex Ch. Susie) whelped on (date).

Conditions of sale: The buyer will pay the sum of ($) at the time of purchase; OR the buyer will pay ($) at the time of purchase and so much per month. AKC registration will be given when the purchase price has been met; OR the buyer will pay ($) and will agree to co-own the puppy with the breeder for a period of time (or permanently).

The seller guarantees the puppy to be in good health at the time of sale and to be free of discernable hereditary defects. The puppy is to be examined by a veterinarian of the buyer's choice within 48 hours of sale and if the veterinarian finds that the puppy is ill or defective it will be returned to the seller immediately. (A full refund will be given or another puppy from the same litter will be exchanged.)

The seller will provide full AKC registration documents and a three-generation pedigree at the time of sale.

The buyer agrees that in the event they are unable to keep the puppy, the seller will be notified and given the option to buy or place the puppy in another home. (This stipulation will continue throughout the life of the dog.)

The buyer agrees never to use this dog in any manner that would be detrimental to the breed.

NOTE: If the dog is sold or given with a limited AKC registration it cannot be used for breeding and cannot be shown in conformation. A stipulation to this effect should be included in the contract.

Another optional clause is the spay/neuter contract, in which no registration papers are given until the dog is either spayed or neutered, should the breeder feel this is in the best interests of the dog.

CONTRACT FOR CO-OWNERSHIPS

Co-ownership contracts vary tremendously, according to the conditions that are worked out between the parties. Some of the items that should be considered are:

- Who keeps and maintains the animal?
- Who pays for daily upkeep and maintenance? How are these expenses, including medical expenses, divided?
- Who shows the dog? Who pays the entry fees? If a handler is employed, who pays the handler? If the dog is Specialed, who pays for the additional expenses, such as travel, advertising, bonuses for the handler?
- If it is a dog, who handles the stud services and how are stud fees divided? If it is a bitch, who chooses the sire, whelps the litter, sells the puppies? Who gets pick of the litter?

Whatever contingencies the two or more co-owners can think of should be included in the contract in order to avoid misunderstandings later on.

STUD SERVICE CONTRACT

The owners of the stud agree to accept a bitch for service by their dog in return for the fee of ($) which is to be paid

(a) At the time of service

(b) Half at the time of service and half when the puppies are born

(c) When the registration papers are presented for signature prior to being sent to the AKC

(d) Upon the birth of (two) live puppies

(e) Stud fee shall be pick of the litter to be selected at the age of (10) weeks

The owner of the bitch agrees to pay travel expenses to and from the home of the stud dog and any boarding expenses which may be incurred during her stay.

The owner of the stud agrees to provide two services to the bitch. If the bitch does not conceive no stud fee is required (or, half the stud fee is required) and a return service will be given.

Prior to the arrival of the bitch in heat proof of negative tests for brucellosis (and any other sexually transmitted diseases which the owner of the stud requires) must be submitted, signed by a veterinarian. (If applicable) proof of the absence of any breed-specific inheritable defects must be provided. Examples of this would be certification by OFA for hips and eye registries for eye diseases.

It is the responsibility of the stud dog owners to maintain the bitch in a clean and healthy environment, and the responsibility of the owners of the bitch to send her in a healthy and clean condition.

ORGANIZATION OF A DOG SHOW

BEST IN SHOW

GROUP COMPETITION

Sporting/Hound/Working/Terrier/Toy/Non-Sporting/Herding

BREED COMPETITION

Best of Breed

Best of Opposite Sex

Best of Winners

Winners Dog

Regular Classes

- Open Dog
- American Bred Dog
- Bred by Exhibitor Dog
- Novice Dog
- Puppy Dog

Winners Bitch

Regular Classes

- Open Bitch
- American Bred Bitch
- Bred by Exhibitor Bitch
- Novice Bitch
- Puppy Bitch

OFFICIAL AMERICAN KENNEL CLUB ENTRY FORM

A

I ENCLOSE $ . . . B . . for entry fees

IMPORTANT—Read Carefully Instructions on Reverse Side Before Filling Out. Numbers in the boxes indicate sections of the instructions relevant to the information needed in that box (PLEASE PRINT)

BREED C	VARIETY [1] D	SEX E
DOG [2] [3] SHOW CLASS F	CLASS [ ] DIVISION Weight color etc G	
ADDITIONAL CLASSES H	OBEDIENCE TRIAL CLASS I	JR SHOWMANSHIP CLASS J

NAME OF (See Back) JUNIOR HANDLER (if any) K

FULL NAME OF DOG L

[ ] AKC REG NO [ ] AKC LITTER NO [ ] ILP NO [ ] FOREIGN REG NO & COUNTRY — Enter number here M	DATE OF BIRTH N PLACE OF BIRTH [ ] USA [ ] Canada [ ] Foreign O Do not print the above in catalog

BREEDER P

SIRE Q

DAM R

ACTUAL OWNER(S) [4] S ______ (Please Print)

OWNER'S ADDRESS ______

CITY ______ STATE ______ ZIP ______

NAME OF OWNERS AGENT (IF ANY) AT THE SHOW T ______

I CERTIFY that I am the actual owner of the dog, or that I am the duly authorized agent of the actual owner whose name I have entered above. In consideration of the acceptance of this entry, I (we) agree to abide by the rules and regulations of The American Kennel Club in effect at the time of this show or obedience trial, and by any additional rules and regulations appearing in the premium list for this show or obedience trial or both, and further agree to be bound by the "Agreement" printed on the reverse side of this entry form. I (we) certify and represent that the dog entered is not a hazard to persons or other dogs. This entry is submitted for acceptance on the foregoing representation and agreement.

SIGNATURE of owner or his agent duly authorized to make this entry U ______

TELEPHONE # ______ V ______

Single copies of the latest editions of the "Rules Applying to "Registration and Dog Shows" and "Obedience Regulations" may be obtained WITHOUT CHARGE from any Superintendent at any show where they are superintending or from THE AMERICAN KENNEL CLUB, 51 MADISON AVENUE, NEW YORK, N.Y. 10010.

AGREEMENT

I(we) acknowledge that the "Rules Applying to Registration and Dog Shows" and, if this entry is for an Obedience Trial, the "Obedience Regulations," have been made available to me (us), and that I am (we are) familiar with their contents. I (we) agree that the club holding this show or obedience trial has the right to refuse this entry for cause which the club shall deem to be sufficient. In consideration of the acceptance of this entry and of the holding of the show or obedience trial and of the opportunity to have the dog judged and to win prize money, ribbons, or trophies, I(we) agree to hold this club, its members, directors, governors, officers, agents, superintendents or show secretary and the owner or lessor of the premises and any employees of the aforementioned parties, harmless from any claim for loss or injury which may be alleged to have been caused directly or indirectly to any person or thing by the act of this dog while in or upon the show or obedience trial premises or grounds or near any entrance thereto, and I(we) personally assume all responsibility and liability for any such claim; and I(we) further agree to hold the aforementioned parties harmless from any claim for loss of this dog by disappearance, theft, death or otherwise, and from any claim for damage or injury to the dog, whether such loss, disappearance, theft, damage, or injury, be caused or alleged to be caused by the negligence of the club or any of the parties aforementioned, or by the negligence of any other person, or any other cause or causes.

I(we) hereby assume the sole responsibility for and agree to indemnify and save the aforementioned parties harmless from any and all loss and expense (including legal fees) by reason of the liability imposed by law upon any of the aforementioned parties for damage because of bodily injuries, including death at any time resulting therefrom, sustained by any person or persons, including myself (ourselves), or on account of damage to property, arising out of or in consequence of my (our) participation in this show or obedience trial, howsoever such injuries, death or damage to property may be caused, and whether or not the same may have been caused or may be alleged to have been caused by negligence of the aforementioned parties or any of their employees or agents, or any other persons.

INSTRUCTIONS

1. (Variety) if you are entering a dog of a breed in which there are varieties for show purposes, please designate the particular variety you are entering, i.e., Cocker Spaniel (solid color black, ASCOB, parti-color), Beagles (not exceeding 13 in. over 13 in. but not exceeding 15 in.), Dachshunds (longhaired, smooth, wirehaired), Collies (rough, smooth), Bull Terriers (colored, white), Manchester Terriers (standard, toy), Chihuahuas (smooth coat, long coat), English Toy Spaniels (King Charles and Ruby, Blenheim and Prince Charles), Poodles (toy, miniature, standard).

2. The following categories of dogs may be entered and shown in Best of Breed competition: Dogs that are Champions of Record and dogs which, according to their owners' records, have completed the requirements for a championship, but whose championships are unconfirmed. The showing of unconfirmed Champions in Best of Breed competition is limited to a period of 90 days from the date of the show where the dog completed the requirements for a championship.

3. (Dog Show Class) Consult the classification in this premium list. If the dog show class in which you are entering your dog is divided, then, in addition to designating the class, specify the particular division of the class in which you are entering your dog, i.e., age division, color division, weight division.

4. A dog must be entered in the name of the person who actually owned it at the time entries for a show closed. If a registered dog has been acquired by a new owner it must be entered in the name of its new owner in any show for which entries closed after the date of acquirement, regardless of whether the new owner has received the registration certificate indicating that the dog is recorded in his name. State on entry form whether transfer application has been mailed to A.K.C. (For complete rule refer to Chapter 14, Section 3.)

If this entry is for Jr Showmanship please give the following information:

JR'S DATE OF BIRTH ______________

JUNIOR SHOWMANSHIP

W

ADDRESS ______________________________

CITY ______________ STATE ______________ ZIP ______________

If Jr Handler is not the owner of the dog identified on the face of this form, what is the relationship of the Jr Handler to the owner?

OFFICIAL AMERICAN KENNEL CLUB ENTRY FORM

(These are standard for all shows)

A. The name of the show-giving club and the date must be listed here.

B. State the amount enclosed for entry fees. Each dog entered must have a separate entry form, but a dog entered in more than one class, for instance sweepstakes and regular classes, is listed on the same form.

C. Name the breed here.

D. Name the variety here, if yours is a breed which is categorized by more than one variety. Dachshunds would be an example.

E. State dog or bitch here.

F. Name the class here, such as Puppy Dog, Novice Dog, etc. Be sure to put Dog or Bitch after the class name.

G. If the puppy class is divided into 6–9, 9–12 months, list the proper category here. If your breed is one which divides classes by color, weight or other breed characteristics, list that here.

H. Additional classes for the same dog, such as sweepstakes or Veterans and Best of Breed, list here. According to AKC rules, a dog which is entered in more than one class, not including sweepstakes, must win the first in order to be eligible to compete in the next. For instance, if a dog is entered in Veterans and Best of Breed, it must win the Veteran class in order to be able to compete in Best of Breed competition. Generally, dogs are not entered in more than one class at a show.

I. Obedience Trial competitors enter here.

J. Junior showmanship enters here. State the class to be entered.

K. Name the junior who will be showing the dog.

L. State the full name of the dog as it appears on the AKC registration certificate.

M. Mark off the correct box and list the complete AKC number.

AKC registration number. The individual registration number assigned to each dog.

AKC litter number. A dog may be shown under its litter number for 30 days after the first show in which it has been shown under a litter number if the individual registration has not been processed. It cannot enter subsequent shows under a litter number.

ILP number. Indeterminate listing privilege. This applies to animals whose parents are unknown or unregisterable, but who are purebred. These are eligible to compete in Obedience Trials only.

Foreign registry. This applies to dogs bred outside the United States, including Canada, Mexico, Bermuda and any other country.

N. List date of birth.

O. List place of birth.

P. List breeder (if more than one list them all).

Q. List full name of sire as registered, including titles, if any.

R. List full name of dam as registered, including titles, if any.

S. State name of the owners at the time the entry form is filled out. If you purchased your dog from the previous owner before the entry for a show closed you can enter the dog in your name provided that transfer-of-ownership papers have been sent to the AKC and that you state this on the entry form.

T. If you employ a handler, list the name here.

U. Sign your name, or, if the handler/agent makes the entry, he or she signs the form for you.

V. List your telephone number, so that if there is a problem with your entry the show Secretary or the Superintendent can reach you. They do not always oblige, but sometimes they do.

W. Fill this in for your junior. Juniors can only show their own dog or one that belongs to a member of the immediate family. Sometimes a family friend will co-own a dog with a junior so that the child can show in junior showmanship.

Glossary

All-breed Club: A group of fanciers from different dog breeds organized into a club to protect and promote the interests of purebred dogs.

American Kennel Club (AKC): The major governing organization for purebred dog activities in the United States. This authoritative registry for purebred dogs is located at 51 Madison Avenue, New York, NY 10010

Bait: The tidbit or treat used to attract a dog's attention in the show ring.

Benched Show: A show in which dogs must be displayed to the public in stalls, called benches, during certain designated hours.

Best in Show: The award given to a dog who defeats all other dogs entered in a show. This designation is only given at all-breed shows.

Best of Breed: The award given to a dog who defeats all other dogs of its breed at a show.

Best of Winners: The award given to either the Winners Dog or the Winners Bitch in each breed at a show.

Bitch: The female of the species.

Catalog: The listing of all dogs entered in a show on any particular day. The catalog contains the judging panel, time schedules, point schedules, owners, breeders and handlers, birth date, addresses of the owners and advertising.

Champion: Title conferred upon a dog who completes the AKC requirements of earning fifteen points, including two shows at which three points or more are awarded.

Conformation: The appearance of a dog, including its anatomical features, way of moving and general physical attributes.

Coronavirus: A virus of the intestinal tract that causes varying degrees of enteritis, vomiting and diarrhea.

Craniomandibular Osteopathy: A genetic disorder affecting the jawbones, causing pain, inflammation and malformation of the jaws.

Dam: Mother of the puppies.

Distemper: A virus that affects many systems in the body, particularly of young puppies. It is characterized by fever, runny nose and malaise and eventually affects the central nervous system. It is usually fatal in puppies, but is controlled by vaccinations.

Dog Handlers Guild: A professional organization of dog handlers and agents, operating primarily in the Midwest.

Dwarfism: A genetic abnormality that causes malformation of the long bones of the legs. The bones fail to grow properly, are misshapen and abnormally short.

External Parasites: Parasites such as fleas and ticks that attack dogs, causing a variety of skin and systemic problems.

Gait: The dog in motion, involving the way it moves as it walks or trots.

Groups: The seven categories of dogs recognized by the AKC—Sporting, Hound, Terrier, Working, Toy, Non-Sporting, and Herding.

Hepatitis: An inflammation of the liver, characterized by fever, malaise and gastrointestinal symptoms, followed by jaundice. It is one of the diseases against which puppies are vaccinated.

Hip Dysplasia: An hereditary condition in which there is excess laxity of the hip joint, eventually causing lameness and/or arthritic changes.

Hypertrophic Osteodystrophy (HOD): An inflammation of unknown origin affecting the long bones of growing dogs. It is usually seen in large and giant breeds and in most cases is self-limiting. In severe cases it causes deformities of the affected limbs.

Internal Parasites: Parasites, such as worms, bacteria or spirochetes, that invade the intestinal tract, or other tissues, in the dog, causing a variety of symptoms and illness, some of which may be severe or even fatal if left untreated.

Judging Schedule: The listing for every show of all judges, the breeds they are scheduled to judge, the numbers of dogs of each breed entered, the ring numbers and the estimated times each breed is to be judged.

Junior Showmanship: Classes held at dog shows for children between the ages of ten and eighteen. Classes are divided according to age and experience.

Kennel Blind: A term used to describe breeders who cannot recognize faults in their dogs, or who think their dogs are always better than their competitors.

Kennel Cough: A contagious, usually mild, upper respiratory disease of dogs. Dogs kept in kennels or confined at dog shows are particularly susceptible to catching kennel cough. There is a vaccination that can be given to minimize the risk.

Leptospirosis: A serious infectious disease whose symptoms may be lymphocytic meningitis, hepatitis and nephritis. It is one of those against which all dogs should be immunized.

Lyme Disease: A disease carried by a spirochete and transmitted through the bite of a deer tick. It can cause fever, lameness, heart, lung or nervous system problems, and over the long term if left untreated will cause arthritis in the joints.

Match Show: A show that carries no championship points but is organized in the same manner as a point show. Match shows are used to provide opportunities for novice owners and novice dogs to learn about dog shows.

Osteochondrosis: A disease of the growth centers of the bone, usually affecting the ends of the bone, found usually in large breed dogs. It is often self-limiting, but may respond to treatment. Occasionally surgery is required to repair damage to cartilage.

Panosteitis: Inflammation of the bones, sometimes called shifting leg lameness because it seems to travel from one leg to another. It affects growing dogs, is usually self-limiting and comes from an unknown cause. Rest and palliative medication is usually recommended.

Parainfluenza: An acute viral infection of the respiratory tract. Vaccination is recommended to prevent puppies from contracting this disease.

Parent Club: The national organization representing fanciers of any particular breed. Most Parent clubs are members of the American Kennel Club and are represented there by an elected Delegate.

Parvovirus: A severe gastrointestinal virus that if left untreated can result in death. In young puppies the virus can lead to lasting damage to the heart.

Parvovirus was first recognized in 1978, and through the dedication of breeders and veterinary scientists, a vaccination was developed that has greatly reduced its incidence in the canine population.

Point Schedule: The number of points awarded at any show determined by the number of entries actually competing. The AKC has divided the United States into nine regions for the purposes of equably distributing points depending upon the number of shows in an area. The point schedule is revised every May to reflect the entries at shows the previous year.

Point Show: An all-breed or Specialty show at which championship points are awarded.

Premium List: Entry information sent by every show-giving club to people who might be interested in attending their show. The premium list may be sent by the club Secretary, or by a professional show Superintendent, who keeps an extensive mailing list. The entry form must contain the following information: date, place, time, judging panel, classes offered, prizes offered, fees and entry blanks. Any additional attractions offered by the club, such as exhibitions or entertainment, may be included in the premium list.

Professional Handlers Association (PHA): An organization of professional handlers, who by virtue of experience and tenure have qualified to be accepted to membership.

Rocky Mountain Spotted Fever: A tick-borne disease, most often found in the western United States, but sometimes seen in the East. This disease causes fever, malaise, depression, seizures and occasionally coma and death. Antibiotic treatment, if begun early, is usually successful in combating this disease.

Sire: Father of the puppies.

Special: Term used to describe a dog or a bitch who has completed its championship title and is in competition for Best of Breed.

Specialing: Term used for a champion who is being regularly shown in Best of Breed competition.

Specialty Club: A club devoted to the protection and promotion of one breed of dog.

Stack: Term used to describe the show pose required of the dog in the ring.

Steward: A ring official whose job it is to assist the judge.

Sweepstakes: Classes offered by Specialty clubs for puppies from the age of six months to eighteen months, in which the entry fees are divided among the winners of the classes according to the number of entries.

Unbenched: A show at which exhibitors are required to be present only during the judging of the class and at which there is no area set aside for the display of any entrants.

Winners Bitch: The award given to the bitch who defeats all nonchampion bitch competitors in the classes.

Winners Dog: The award given to the dog who defeats all nonchampion dog competitors in the classes.